Chai & Chapati

MY TIME IN THE PUNJAB

Peter O'Neil

ISBN: 1518789099

ISBN 13: 9781518789090

Dedication

To my students—past, present, and future. I have had the privilege of serving over twenty-five hundred of you over the past twenty-six years. Your smiles, humor, energy, ideas, and kindness have made, and continue to make, my career a joy and my life fulfilling.

To all the people around the world who have invited me into their homes, their cultures, and their hearts.

In particular, I dedicate this book to my friends from the Punjab.

Namaste.

Contents

Acknowledgments

I'd like to thank all of my friends and family for encouraging me throughout the years to put my travel experiences on paper. A special shout-out to some of my friends and family for helping me with the initial construction and editing of this book: Kevin Diehl, Lenny Witham, Lee Boyan, Miriam Boyajian, Lisa Witham, Lin Lawson, Sarah Erickson, and Bill O'Neil. Thank you to Maureen Cullen, Tricia Apel, Barb Sirotin, Kathy Bader, and Bob Hetzel for making the experience possible. Also, a big thank-you to the team at CreateSpace for polishing the finished product.

Preface

India is a land of opposites. Anything that can be said about India, the opposite can also be said. What is described here is one person's experience, in one part of the country, at one moment in time. The opposite can be said about everything described in this book. Like the fabled blind men who tried to describe an elephant by the part to which they had access, this description in no way can ever describe the mosaic of our incredible Mother India.

Chapter One

I had never planned on working in, let alone visiting, India. People had told me it was filthy, chaotic, unbearably hot, and polluted. Did I need that at this time of my life? Already, I had seen and experienced more of the world than most, thanks to teaching in international schools, and I was comfortably settled in the most agreeable climate in the United States for me: that of South Florida. In Fort Lauderdale, I had found a teaching position in a local public school, and I was intent upon "building my garden" there. All was good.

Mid–school year this changed when my friend Eileen called me from India. We had worked together at an American school in Cairo and had become close friends. After Cairo, she had chosen to remain overseas, while I chose to return home. She called to tell me about an available math position at her new post in New Delhi. She told me the pay and benefits were excellent and that yearly flights to home and the cost of storing my furniture would be covered; a generous shipping allowance was also part of the package. Even better, her principal would be traveling to Florida over the winter holidays and would be able to interview me in person. This sounded too good to be true.

Eileen and about six other teachers who had worked with us in Cairo were working in India at the time, so I would have a ready-made group of pals with whom I could play. How could I not have accepted that offer? I had already worked in Venezuela, Cameroon, Paris, and Egypt, and I had studied for a year in Wales, totaling seven years overseas. People would ask me when I was going to try Asia, and I would tell them I was saving that for my next lifetime. But now I found myself accepting a job overseas again, this time in incredible India.

Chapter Two

It was September of my second school year in India. I'd had a good first year but pretty much stayed in Delhi and focused on my job. On holidays, I had traveled outside of India. But this was my second year, and I was determined to see more of New Delhi at least.

We had only a half day of school due to parent conferences, and I thought I would take that opportunity to explore the city. I had never been to Delhi's zoo, and it wasn't far from the school, so I thought I'd stop there on my way home. And heck, it was Friday after all. I knew from the previous year and my experiences working in other countries that falling into the habit of heading straight home from work was not going to help me reach my goal of learning about my host country. I loved my job, but while on campus, I could have been at any private school in America. We had baseball, basketball, cheerleaders, and *Fiddler on the Roof* as the spring musical, and all my colleagues spoke English with an American accent. The television commercials advertising "Incredible India" made me feel guilty. Here I was living in India and found myself stuck in the same working grind as I was back home in the United States. Was this what happened when you reached your forties? Was I losing my sense of adventure?

I left the campus around one o'clock and walked to the neighborhood taxi stand. Unique to India are the Ambassador taxis. They look like a car from the forties or fifties, something you might find surviving in Havana, Cuba. But these cars are different, in that they have a distinctively British feel to them, like the Aston Martin that James Bond drove. The Ambassadors are larger and clunkier but have the same curves. Despite their hackney look, they are proudly Indian-designed and manufactured. At one time, I'm sure the Ambassadors were elegant, but their elegance had faded since then; they were missing various parts, and their seat covers were in need of repair. Some drivers put in lace curtains or other accoutrements to personalize their cab. Delhi did have air-conditioned taxis that could be hired, but the price for those taxis would be double, and who wanted to wait in the one-hundred-degree heat for it to arrive when the Ambassadors were ready to go at the taxi stand?

This Ambassador was rickety, but the driver was pleasant, recently up from a nap on a cot at the taxi stand. The taxi drivers often lived at these outdoor stands, and it was common to see them sleep, bath, and eat there. These guys knew me, as I lived off campus and took a taxi to and from the school every day. Generally, the teachers who had families lived within the walled campus, and the single folks lived off campus, the single males living farthest away. Living off campus in an Indian neighborhood was fine by me. I loved learning about cultures, and India had many from which to choose! There were certain drivers who would make conversation with their broken English and others who would remain quiet the entire time. They took turns in taking customers, and I was generally happy with any cab. I just hoped it wasn't a certain man who always had terrible body odor. I was lucky that day; there was no need for me to purchase a lei of marigolds to mask any smells.

I noticed that the backseat doors had no handles to roll down the windows. I had seen this before and knew the routine. I asked the driver if I could roll down the backseat windows, as this was the hottest time of day, and a cross breeze would make up for the lack of air conditioning. He handed me the handle over his shoulder, and I fitted it in the exposed gear shaft on the door and rolled the window down. I leaned over to do the same on the other door before returning the handle to him.

On the fifteen-minute drive from the school to the zoo, we passed the many embassies along the way. Next to the crowded and chaotic "old" Delhi, New Delhi sat as India's British-planned capital. New Delhi was filled with roundabouts that added an elegance and British feel to the capital. New Delhi could be considered one of Asia's most beautiful capitals: organized, tree-lined streets, and broad roadways that lead to monuments or important government buildings. It did have its draw-backs, including occasional slums peppered throughout. Often the slums evolved from a temporary camp for the workers who built the buildings. It was very difficult to remove the workers once the buildings were complet-ed. Local politicians would jump in and represent them in town meetings, defending their rights, and in turn get their votes. Those are the workings of the largest democracy in the world.

The city's skies were forever hazy, making a clear-sky day a special treat. While regulations officially forbade cows from roaming the streets, they were rarely enforced in most areas. However, New Delhi was an ex-ception. In British colonial cities, it was typical to have a major boulevard called the "King's Way." I liked how the Indians had changed the name to "Rajpath" after gaining independence from the United Kingdom (*raj* be-ing what rulers were called). They even added a street called "Janpath," which translates to "the people's way." As New Delhi and Delhi were one big metropolis to me, I used their names interchangeably to describe where I lived.

I enjoyed seeing the flags on the various mansions and guessing which country's embassy resided on that property. I especially enjoyed passing the embassies of those countries where I had lived in the past: Cameroon, Venezuela, Egypt, the UK, and France. I had a connection to each of those places, and my heart longed for the times I had spent in each country and some of the people I knew there.

I felt the same thing every time I watched the Olympic parade of na-tions on television. Tears would actually come to my eyes while watching Cameroon's few Olympians pass by. I knew how difficult it would be for Cameroonians to get from their village to the Olympic arena. One year the station did a commercial break right after the extensive Canadian team entered. I was devastated. Cameroon follows Canada, and its entrance was not televised due to the commercial. I wondered if I would have the same longing for India after completing this two-year contract.

We arrived, and when I got out of the taxi, I realized the zoo was closed on Fridays. The driver asked if he could take me somewhere else.

I leaned away from the cab and thought about it for a moment. I wished I had brought my *Lonely Planet* book with me. Delhi had many sights to see, but I couldn't think of one at the moment. To my right I saw a line of people entering a historic site next door, Purana Qila, the ruins of the ramparts of a mid-sixteenth-century fort. I had driven by the other side of it, which flanks the Yamuna River, many times. I was told that these days it was just a well-maintained park with lakes and some amusements for children. I was there anyway; why not just go in? I told the taxi driver my plan and entered the ticket line. I paid (what was to me) the ridiculously cheap admission fee, the equivalent of about ten cents, and entered the park.

After walking up an inclined path, I reached a large, flat expanse of grass with occasional groupings of trees dotted throughout. I could see why it would make an ideal place for a fort. I seemed to be on the top of a small, flat hill. Indians cherished the green parks they had in their city as a welcome respite from the traffic and chaos. Some families were strolling along the path. I thought how nice it was to see three generations of the family together. On the grass were small groups or couples chatting or reclining. It was a large park, but it did not seem crowded at all, perhaps due to the admission fee. This large, protected expanse of grass once had served as one of the refugee camps for Indian Muslims waiting to be moved to the newly created Pakistan during the years of partition. I wondered if the folks enjoying it that day were aware of its important historical significance.

I had been following the path outlining the perimeter for about a block when I noticed a group of young men sitting in a circle on the grass under a tree, watching me. They smiled and waved to me, and I waved back, but I continued on my way. I appreciated the friendliness and curiosity of Indians. With my blue eyes, fair skin, and shaved head, I stuck out from the crowd. Then I heard one of them say, "Please, come here," while the others motioned with their hands for me to join them. They probably didn't expect me to accept, as tourists and foreigners usually kept to themselves and to their tight itineraries. And besides, Purana Qila would typically not be on the "must-see" list of tourists stopping in Delhi on their way to the bigger sights like the Taj Mahal.

However, I was not a tourist in the normal sense, and they seemed friendly enough, so I accepted their invitation. I walked over to the group and could see the smiles on their faces getting bigger and also some growing nervousness from them as they sat up straighter. One of them awkwardly blurted, "What's your name?" I responded, and they politely invited me to join their semicircle on the grass, and I did. Their smiles grew even bigger. Then transpired what typically happens when expats meet folks who don't speak much English. Each attempted a few phrases they learned in school. "Where are you from? Why are you here?" Between each of these sentences they spoke in Hindi among themselves, giggling. Their smiles showed their successes, payoffs for the hours they had studied this foreign language in school. It was as if they had thrown wet spaghetti on the wall and it had actually stuck.

Their language, Hindi, is the most widely spoken language in India. I was surprised to learn that it's actually in the family of European languages, or more correctly, Indo-European languages. One way to tell if a language is in the Indo-European family is by how the numbers two and ten are pronounced. If two and ten begin with a *d* or *t* sound, it's likely in the Indo-European family—for example, *dos* and *diez* in Spanish, *deux* and *dix* in French, *two* and *ten*, and so on. In Hindi, it's *do* and *das*. While *d* and *t* are different, they require the same tongue position in the mouth. Test it yourself. While northern Indians might have very different coloring from Europeans, they, along with Persians, are actually closer cousins to Europeans than Jews and Arabs.

English was required after a certain age in Indian schooling, but the quality of instruction varied greatly. Sadly, much of the population in northern India was not functional in English despite many years of study. Hindi is a northern Indian language and is the most popularly known language in the country. It's script, Devanagari, is also the script used for the Sanskrit language of the Hindu religious texts. As in many of the former British colonies, when the imperial rulers left, they left their language but few who could model it. Because of that, the locals speak with heavy accents and use some interesting turns of phrases. An Indian friend in Delhi once asked me what I did on Sundays. After I explained what I typically did, I asked what he did. He told me he would stop by the homes of his friends, have some tea, and do some leg pulling. I smiled and asked, "Leg pulling?"

"We tell jokes to and about one another."

I smiled again.

Southern Indians are known to have a higher percentage of English speakers. Many in the south prefer English, as opposed to Hindi, to be India's lingua franca. There are a lot of political discussions behind this sentiment. Southern Indians feel their languages aren't given the same weight as the northern-originated Hindi. Southern India has even started its own films in languages of the region to challenge the Hindi predominance in Bollywood. Southern Indians thus tend to have stronger English skills. This might explain why so many of the international call centers are based in southern India rather than in northern India.

After a few more formal questions from the young men, I noticed their eyes darting off behind me. I turned my head and saw that I was being upstaged by a romantic couple necking on the grass. I then understood why the young men had chosen this spot. India is a very traditional society. Guys hang out with guys, and girls with girls. Premarital relations are difficult. I could understand why a kissing couple on the grass would be a spectacle of interest for these men in their twenties.

As their questions began to wane, I thought I'd reciprocate. I wanted to know their names, where they were from, and how they knew one another. The tallest of the five young men was named Dhruv, and he did most of the responding. While his English was broken, it was the best in the group. He said they were friends, but actually like cousins. They were from a small town in Haryana, the state just south of Delhi. They all had the same surname: Kassana. I had never heard of Haryana, but in the previous years, it apparently broke off, along with Delhi, from the larger and more well-known state of Punjab. The name "Punjab" translates to "the land of the five rivers." They told me they had taken the train up to Delhi for the day to get out of the village, to spend some time away from their family, and to enjoy this particular park. They would be returning to their village that evening.

The questions changed to their curiosity about studying in America and how to get into the business schools there. They asked about the best schools, the best majors to study, and what the costs would be. I tried to answer their questions the best that I could, but I guess they could see it wasn't my field of expertise. Needing a change of environment, Naveen stood up and asked, "Peter, you walk with us?"

Naveen appeared to be the leader among them. Naveen walked like a leader, his chest leading his body. Later I would learn that his father had been serving in the military. Perhaps his father had instilled the healthy habit of morning push-ups. I had a good feeling about these guys, and I figured this would be a nice way to learn about their culture, so I accepted Naveen's invitation.

Chapter Three

On our walk, my new acquaintances each continued to try a few phrases of English with me, always smiling and speaking among themselves in Hindi afterward. The second-best English speaker's name was Ravi. He had a sweetness to him and seemed more innocent than the others. From their interactions, I sensed he was kidded for that attribute. He seemed to be speaking purely from his heart. We slowly walked on the perimeter path, each of the guys taking turns at my side, often putting an arm around my shoulder. Another guy named Manish picked a dandelion flower from the grass and handed it to me with his head tilted to one side. "For you, Peter." Oh my. How sweet. Are these guys for real? Do men in India normally give flowers to one another, or was this just their way of entertaining me?

Manish was skin and bones. His face was less symmetric than his cousins', and he had a strong, if slightly crooked, nose bridge. From our discussion on the grass, I got the impression that he didn't have grand dreams of studying abroad. I imagined him a dutiful son who enjoyed his family and the village life. He seemed surprised that I would be spending time with them but quickly got comfortable with the idea and with me.

We stopped at the farthest point of the park and rested our hands on the stone rampart to take in the view. We could see the other remnants of India's glorious past in the distance, from the round domes of various shrines to the deceased Muslim rulers. The minarets from Nizamuddin, the historic and present-day Sufi Muslim quarter, caught my eye. The trees appeared dry and less lush than what could be seen in the south of India. Perhaps that was due to the semidesert climate of northern India. The landmarks poked out of these dusty trees. I pointed to a few prominent ones, like Humayun's Tomb, but the guys didn't seem to know their historical significance. I knew about it because that particular tomb is on every tourist's "must see" itinerary. I remembered that my tour guide at Humayun's Tomb pointed to Purana Qila and said that Humayun, the great leader of that era, grew up in that fort. I would check my tour book or the Internet when I got back to my apartment to see if my memory was correct.

I hadn't seen Delhi from that height before, and I was happy to be walking with them. Naveen asked if I had a camera. I pulled it from my school bag, and Ravi got his hands on it first and dodged the others like a football player intercepting the ball. I wasn't used to things being pulled from my hand, and I hoped he'd be careful with it. Giving up some of my control took some restraint, but I began to trust these guys more and more. Ravi started arranging us for group photos, all the while keeping the camera out of the hands of the others, who were anxious to snap one themselves. We semihuddled, arms draped around one another. The cousins smiled brightly and seemed very happy to be taking a photo with me.

When looking at the photos later on my computer, I wondered how they kept their teeth so white. I saw how gracefully their single-toned brown hands hung off the shoulders of their friends. Any one of them could have been a hand model. They had thin wrists, and their hands were large and angular, with no puffiness or roundness. On all their wrists were the string bracelets, or *rakhi*, which they wore until they disintegrated. The thread could be any color, but red predominated. Sometimes the rakhis were on one wrist, sometimes both, and often there were several rakhis on one wrist. They could have knots separating shells, or beads, or nothing at all. I assumed there was a significance to the bracelets, as Hinduism has much symbolism. Maybe I was reading too much into them. They were likely leftovers from Raksha Bandhan, the Hindu holiday celebrating the bond between brothers and sisters. Sisters will tie a threaded bracelet on their brother's wrist as a symbol of the bond between them and as a symbol of their brother's responsibility in protecting them. I thought how nice it was that even schools closed on this unique holiday that celebrates siblings. I grew up with three sisters, and we were extremely close. I wished that had been a yearly, formal ritual for us as kids. I added that to the list of Indian rituals that I admired.

These "Haryana cousins," as I later referred to my friends, seemed so joyful and were quite the jokesters among themselves. They continued to take turns pulling a bloom from the grass or shrub and putting it in front of me with the same "Peter, for you." After several rounds of this, Naveen took a scrappy branch with no leaves or blooms and handed it to me. "Peter, for you!" he said. This caused even more rounds of laughter, each one bending over to catch his breath. These guys knew how to create fun out of nothing.

When Naveen spoke in English to me, he tilted his head downward, leaned toward me, and spoke carefully and gently, taking the time to find the correct word. My guess is that he'd had very little practice speaking English with a native. The best part of Naveen's English was that he knew enough to include verbs!

When I had accepted the job in Delhi, I had just assumed that in a former British colony, English would be everywhere. I was wrong. Manish asked, "Peter, cell phone?" Dropping the verb, among other words, was the easiest way to communicate for Manish. Before I could finish taking the mobile out of my pocket, like my camera, it was in his hands, and he was typing his contact information in it. The others grabbed it from him to do the same.

Rohit was the quiet, shy one, who knew the least amount of English. Ravi said he was a very good fighter/wrestler. Manish grabbed Rohit's bicep and told me to look. "Big!" he said. The shortest of the men, Rohit, had some meat on his bones. I learned later that these young men came from the Gujjar caste, whose men were known to be the protectors of the raj. Today, many of India's greatest wrestlers come from this caste. I remembered memorizing in my world history class in high school that India had four castes. Since arriving in India, I had been learning that it was more complicated than that because, as I was learning, there were levels within castes. I learned later that these men were from the bottom caste but toward the top of the "Other Backward Classes," as the Indian government labeled it.

Dhruv was the most reserved of the five. He was still delightful, but his mind was sometimes elsewhere. I wondered why. I would guess that women would have found him to be the most attractive of the five. Between his height, winning smile against his dark skin, pronounced jaw-line, and shadow of a beard, he was swarthy indeed. I would learn that he was married, that he and his wife were fourteen when they married, and that they had a young child. I guessed he was about twenty-two now. I wanted to know more about his early marriage, but he didn't seem to want to go there. This excursion with his pals was likely the young adult-hood that he was trying to retain despite being married so early.

We continued our walk on the path, rounding the edge of the fort and then down toward the lagoon. There were paddlers enjoying themselves, skimming across the lake beneath the fort. The guys asked if I wanted to go on a boat ride. Fearing they would offer to pay, I declined. I didn't know their financial situation. I assumed from their humble clothing and their lack of English skills that money was tight. I had heard that the average wage for workers in Delhi was only five dollars per day. While I never felt rich on a teacher's salary in the United States, I did in India. I wasn't going to accept their paying for a boat ride for all of us.

Just after the boat launch, there was a concession stand. "Peter, you drink something?" A fruit soda seemed like the more affordable option to accept from them, so I agreed. I still offered to pay for everyone, but they refused vehemently. We sat in the shade and enjoyed it. I still felt guilty that they had paid. We snapped photos arm over arm, and at this point, we were practically sitting in one another's laps. "Puppy dogs," I thought.

We came a full circle to the entrance, and it was time to bid fare-well. "What a delightful two hours," I thought. I got my mind totally off work and got to spend time with folks who reminded me of the good-ness and wholeness of folks who have fewer material things. These were people who lived closer to the soil and were more interconnected with their extended families. It reinforced my belief that the American culture had lost a lot in its progress.

I'd had a nice time with these guys, but I knew I would likely never see them again. Our worlds were so different. Of course, they were insisting I come to their village sometime to meet their families. I made niceties, saying how much I would enjoy that and that we would have to see about it. They didn't accept that and wouldn't let me leave until I said, "Yes, I will come to your village." I told them that I would "try" to come to their village but knew in my heart that I wouldn't. At that point, I just wanted to get back to my world. Teachers are exhausted on Fridays, and while I had experienced a lovely afternoon, I wanted some quiet time and some control. We walked to the taxi park, and they sent me off with waves and smiles.

As the taxi drove me back to my apartment, I looked out at the Indian faces on the roads with a new perspective. A disheveled little boy, whose hair needed to be cut, approached the taxi with his hand outstretched. The boy came to my window, and I gave my standard sympathetic refusal. The taxi driver didn't offer any coins either, but he looked into the boy's eyes. Next I saw the driver's finger moving a lock of hair on the little boy's face over to the side so he could see his eyes better. It was such a tender, fatherly thing to do. It stuck with me: I'm giving you no money, but I acknowledge you as a person, a child who is still worthy of touch despite your predicament.

Chapter Four

I was back to my routine and was quickly enveloped with work. One of the advantages of working as a teacher is that the workday flies by. The young men I had met in the park were out of sight and, therefore, out of my mind. But that didn't last very long. I was surprised when I began receiving text messages from them. The first few texts were short, in English, and generally said "hello" and that they missed me. Then the texts started coming in Hindi, so I asked Chaya, who taught science next door to me, to translate for me. Although of Indian ethnicity, Chaya had grown up in California. Still, her Hindi was pretty good. I enjoyed stopping by her room before the kids came. She was always willing to help me adjust to the school and answer any questions I had about India. The message from the Kassana cousins apparently contained flowery, loving language of their missing me and more insistence that I come to their village. They wanted to make an exact date for my supposed visit.

I wrote back that I was busy at work and didn't have a car, and I wasn't sure about how to get to the village. However, next time they were in Delhi, we would get together. No, that wasn't good enough. Then they would call, and in their broken English, I could hear in their voices that they truly wanted to show me their village. Well, OK. How could I say "no" to that?

I started to do the research on how I would get to their village. Would I hire a taxi? What would that cost? Was there a train that went there? Finally, I decided to just pay a taxi driver to take me there, to wait four hours, and then to take me back. It would cost about seventy dollars, but at that point, I just needed to satisfy these guys and get it over with. I would do this once and then never again. After all, teaching is exhausting, and I needed my weekends to recuperate, preferably in the air-conditioned comfort of my weekend sanctuary: my clean and orderly apartment. Besides, I didn't speak Hindi, and they didn't really speak English. What would we say to one another for all those hours?

Chapter Five

I arranged for one of my favorite taxi drivers, Mr. Singh, who had taken me to school on several occasions, to take me to the village in Haryana on a certain Saturday. Saturday came, and as I had my morning coffee, I began thinking of ways I could get out of the trip. I could call the guys and tell them I wasn't feeling well. Or I could just not show up. No, I couldn't do that. I called Eileen, whom I had always called when I needed a rational ear, and told her my dilemma. She encouraged me to go for it, and I realized she was right. After all, I had served in the Peace Corps two decades before; I knew how to tolerate heat and hang out in a village. How different could India be from West Africa? For safety, I told Eileen the names of the young men and the name of the village in Haryana. If I wasn't back by evening, then at least she'd know something had happened to me. She gave me confidence that all would work out.

Mr. Singh was in front of my house at 9:00 a.m., just as planned. There were advantages to being in a former British colony: timeliness was one of them. I had already had breakfast and showered and was ready to go. While I would normally wear shorts at home and in my immediate neighborhood, which was accustomed to seeing expats, I reluctantly put on my jeans, knowing I'd be with men who always wore long pants, even in a one-hundred-degree weather. Mr. Singh was an older man and spoke English well. He was curious as to why I was going to this place, a place with no known tourist attractions. I explained about the friends I had made and their invitation. His reaction told me he had never driven an expat on a trip like this.

The drive went through streets I had never been on, and I was able to watch the people of Delhi doing their Saturday-morning routines. Sari-clad women carried milk pails on their heads, school kids walked to classes in their uniforms, other people shopped, and men squatted with their tea in front of shops. In much of the world, it is common to see folks of all ages doing the "third-world squat." I wondered how many of my compatriots could even get into the position, let alone remain there for an extended period with a cup of chai in their hands. No wonder this was the country that introduced yoga to the world.

I was startled seeing women carrying bricks on their heads at construction sites. Why were they dressed so nicely? They had turquoise saris with matching meshed fabric flowing from the top of their heads, which elegantly carried six to eight bricks from a wheelbarrow to a wall. Their children could often be seen walking alongside their mothers while on the job. I learned that the mothers were often widowed and forced to assume the debt of their spouse or their spouse's family as indentured servants. As there was no money for day care, their children came with them to the job. Seeing such a reality of was one of the costs of living in India.

Before long we were beyond the southern part of Delhi and into the rural countryside. As in many parts of northern India, many folks lived along the main road rather than down and away from it. In places like this, you could see the daily theater of India from your car window. Cows sauntered across the road at their convenience, and they got the right-of-way. They often could be seen standing on the median strip, apparently getting a high off the exhaust fumes from the traffic. The cows always looked quite content. I could see people bathing alongside the road, as that was where the water taps were. Bathing is tricky because the bathers are essentially bathing with their clothes on. While men may strip down to some form of undergarment, women remain much more covered. The water soaks through their saris and underclothing, and somehow in the end they are clean.

While nudity is considered immodest and even taboo, another morning ritual is not. People defecating on the side of the road is, unfortunately, a common sight in India. While women are a bit more discreet, men and children are not. Between that, the meandering cows, people walking alongside the road and wanting to cross it, and other distractions, cars were rarely able to clock more than thirty miles an hour, even though we were driving on a highway meant for fifty or sixty miles an hour.

When we were stopped in traffic, I looked over and saw a group of men, this time sitting on crates outside of a teashop, sipping chai. They were wearing loose white pants with matching long-sleeved shirts and light vests. Their faces were brown, and their skin was wrinkled. Topping their heads were bright red turbans with intricate white designs. In India, clothing styles can signify local ethnicity. "We must be close to Rajasthan," I thought, as it was known for these colorful turbans.

After about an hour and forty minutes of driving, we reached the agreed-upon meet-up spot near their village: a bus station. I had to use the bathroom, and I asked the driver where I might go. He pointed to a tile-covered wall with maybe five partitions on either side of the tile wall. The floor slanted toward the wall and created a slight trough. It was likely designed to work with running water, but this had none. Apparently, you were supposed to step into the semiprivate stall and urinate against the tile wall. Pedestrians would only see you from the waist up. I wondered if it was built for women to use too, and, if so, how they would do it. For the moment, I would gladly use my male privilege of standing while I urinated. As I approached the first stall, it became evident from the smell and the flies that several people had defecated there rather than just urinated. Oh boy, what to do? Already, folks were watching me; should I turn around and find a tree later? I glanced in a few of the stalls and found the least disgusting one. When I finished, I looked for a place to wash my hands. That was obviously asking too much, so I wiped them on my jeans and returned to the car.

Chapter Six

Looking up, I saw a small sedan approaching Mr. Singh's taxi. Behind the glass I could see the smiles of the guys I met at the park: Rohit driving, Naveen at his side, Dhruv, Manish, and Ravi in the back. There they were, right on schedule. They got out of the car and gave me hugs, held my hand, and patted my back. They seemed genuinely pleased to see me. They looked at Mr. Singh, tall and slender and wearing nice slacks, a white dress shirt, and a powder-blue sweater. He sported a graying beard, and his head was topped with a white turban. Any Indian who saw him would know he was a Sikh.

The Sikhs are often confused for Muslims outside of India due to their beards and turbans. They're not Muslims, but their religion began during the time of Muslim rule, so some of the Sikh customs mimicked those of their rulers. Sikhism is actually an offshoot of Hinduism. Originally, the Sikhs protected the country from invasions from the northwest. One story described a leader asking all Hindus to send their eldest sons to the most northwesterly state, the Punjab, to serve in the army. As was the case with other castes, their profession evolved into a caste of its own.

They have many unique traditions, one of which is that of the men taking the surname "Singh" (lion) and their wives taking the surname "Kaur" (princess). Sikhs are known for feeding the hungry in their temples and for their gold-enameled temple in Amritsar, Punjab. They are also known as hard workers and are often employed as security guards. Eating meat is not taboo in most Sikh families, as it was encouraged by the army to produce soldiers who were as strong and aggressive as possible (some devout Hindus believe that people in meat-eating cultures are more aggressive and prone to conflict than those who are not).

I'm sure the cousins were worrying about what I would have to pay Mr. Singh for my trip. I explained that I had hired Mr. Singh to wait for me there for four hours, and that he would take me back before evening. The guys protested and said I had to spend the night in the village. I told them I wouldn't be staying the night this time, and I was insistent that I was going home that night. Their faces showed disappointment, but they knew they couldn't win. They made some comments about how expensive it was to take a taxi and that I could've taken a bus. I explained it was not a problem. I really wanted to see them, and the money was worth it. I made an arrangement with Mr. Singh to be back by three o'clock that afternoon.

I stepped into the backseat of Rohit's car with the guys. The fact that we were squashed together in the backseat, of course, was of no importance to them, since they probably often traveled that way. As we pulled away from Mr. Singh, I felt a bit like a kindergartner being dropped off at the first day of school. Mr. Singh, while he didn't know me well, had years of experience working with expats. He at least knew what I was about and might have been a bit concerned seeing me drive off the main road in the backseat of a rickety sedan with five (almost) strangers.

I learned that this was Rohit's family car and that it wasn't always in working order. It was working that day, so we were in good shape. We stopped at a gas station along the main road before heading into the village. Naveen paid for the gasoline, refusing my offer to pay. He bought a large bag of potato chips and a soda that, of course, was shared among all. One grabbed the bag from the other and took more than his fair share, laughing at the others' sense of disappointment. While I tried to politely refuse the chips, I had to accept it in order to avoid explaining that I generally don't eat junk food. When I was offered the soda that they were passing around, I pointed to my water bottle and said I was OK. We turned onto the dirt road that led to the village, when Naveen motioned to Rohit to pull over at a fruit stand. In careful English, he asked, "Peter, you will eat banana?"

"Yes," I said. The bananas were gone in no time, and their skins were tossed out the window.

Beautiful tall trees, perhaps eucalyptus, ran along either side of the dirt road. Through the leaves I could see fields of crops. A trail of dust followed our car, and at that time I knew I was going to leave a lot dustier than when I arrived. Whenever we stopped or slowed down for a dip in the road, the dust would catch up to us and enter the car. I was wishing I had a bandana to cover my mouth. It didn't seem to matter at that point; there was so much laughter and a feeling of "we're all in this together" in the car that the dust became insignificant.

Two of the guys were on either side of me, and, consequently, my elbows rested on their thighs and my shoulders leaned against their chests. Their bodies felt warmer than mine. If these had been American men, we'd have been doing everything in our power not to be resting against one another. Indian men didn't have these hang-ups and were used to sensing the touch, temperature, and scent of the other bodies pressed against them on a regular basis. I started to wonder about the cowboy-machismo burden that American men carried. It is so much work to keep up that image.

There were certain things they wanted to show me in their village, one of which was the Yamuna River. This was the same river that passed through Delhi and was the largest tributary of the "mother" Ganges River. From Delhi, it passed through Haryana and continued through the state of Uttar Pradesh, where it would be photographed by millions next to the Taj Mahal. The Yamuna, named after a goddess, was known to be filthy by the time it met up with the even more sacred river, the Ganges, in Allahabad. Sacred or not, I would not be taking a sip or dip in it that day, as I had seen locals do in Delhi.

To get to the Yamuna, they wanted to take me on motorcycles. We parked the car in the village and mounted three motorcycles, two guys on each. Ravi wanted me on his bike, but Naveen won that battle, and I was directed to mount his bike. I put my hands on Naveen's waist, but soon wrapped my arms around his waist to keep from being ejected onto the bumpy country road. No helmets, but at least I had sunglasses. I had always avoided motorcycles in the past. My sister worked as a nurse in an emergency room and had recounted to me the carnage she saw from motorcycle accidents.

As we traveled on the dusty and bumpy road to the river, I started to ask myself if I had made a big mistake. No helmet, no "expat hospital" nearby, nobody except Eileen knew where I was, and she didn't really know exactly where I was or who these men were. Besides, I really didn't know these guys other than through a polite walk in a park one day and a few words of broken English exchanged. Oh well, I couldn't do anything about it at that point, and I was with Naveen, who seemed like the most responsible of them all. So I decided to give up my need for control and go with my gut feeling of trusting these people.

Along the way, we stopped to speak to a man of their same age who was walking with his father and carrying some farming equipment. This was one of their friends from school, and we chatted for a bit. I say "we," but I mean "they." I shook their hands and smiled and tried to look interested as they spoke in Hindi to one another. As the guys were explaining who I was, I could see the father doing the Indian head wobble. It meant he understood. It always made me smile when I saw Indians do that.

Before we set off again, I pointed over to an onion-domed structure in the distance that looked like a tomb. It seemed strange sitting in the middle of the field, far from Delhi where these popped up everywhere. It looked neglected. Perhaps historians didn't know about it? I love learning history, so I asked Dhruv, who spoke the most English, about it. With an air of annoyance, he said something about "the invaders" and threw his hands down as if it was not important. As I thought about it later, I realized that the structure was part of the Muslim dynasty that had ruled India for hundreds of years. The Muslims left behind beautiful, Persian-influenced architecture, much of which consisted of tombs for their deceased. To this day, tourists spend most of their time visiting the many Muslim sights. I imagine the Hindus must feel visitors are getting a one-sided impression, the victor's impression, of India, a country that has always been Hindu in the majority, despite who was ruling. I figured Dhruv's lack of interest in it had something to do with his being a Hindu.

Delhi has very few Hindu tourist sights to boast of. Recently, a wealthy Hindu built a massive Disneyesque Hindu temple in Delhi called the Swaminarayan Akshardham. I conjectured that part of the reason he may have created it was as a move to balance the scales of Muslim and Hindu tourist sites in the capital. The complex is massive. Imagine the symmetry, gardens, and beauty of the Taj Mahal, but add intricacies in the details of the columns and onion domes. Close up, it becomes truly Hindu as the carvings are of flora, fauna, dancers, musicians, and the many Hindu deities. From a distance, the structures of the complex look like sand castles—each layer, a carefully dropped dab of wet sand. But up close, they look like an artist carefully subtracted dust with a small chisel and a small brush. Outside of the temple were more utilitarian-looking buildings, with displays on India, Hinduism, and this visionary's view of their history. It was in this temple that I learned my most important lesson of Hinduism.

In the museum there was a statue of a rock with a man chiseling himself from it. Very simply, life's dharma (personal work) is to work out your karma (reaction to actions in previous lives) in the hopes of reaching nirvana (heaven). That is, if you want to end the cycle of lifetimes, the goal would be to chisel correctly so you can go to heaven after enduring fewer lifetimes. Interfering with someone's dharma would impede that process. Did that mean that assisting in the relief of poverty or with disease might hurt the sufferers' chances to get to heaven? So, while the Abrahamic-influenced world is charged to help the less fortunate, or at least to feel guilty if they are not helping, what I was learning was that Hindus believed that helping the unfortunate would actually be hurting them. This floored me. Had I interpreted correctly? I had just assumed that helping people outside of your family was human nature, not religiously based.

I remembered what someone had told me about visiting India: "India will shake the foundation of everything you know to be true." I was shaken. I had lived in a village in Cameroon as a Peace Corps volunteer and had seen charity everywhere. Nobody went hungry in my village. There was always enough because there was never too much, as one expat told me there. A decade later I was living in Egypt, where their majority religion, Islam, dictated that all must give a percentage of their income to the poor. But this was India, and I was learning that this huge chunk of humanity was raised to be concerned with one's self, first, and one's family, second. Charity beyond the family was institutionally taught to be harmful to receivers of the charity and therefore discouraged.

The museum had several beautiful reflecting ponds and some shaded areas. I sat down on a granite step and leaned against one of the columns to digest all of these issues. I thought of the parents of my students in Delhi who were working with international aid organizations to eradicate polio, set up microloans, improve the standing of women, and so on. I wondered what Hindus felt about foreign-aid services interfering in the karma of Indians. I would have to carefully ask some Hindus about this.

Back onto the motorbikes. We arrived at the river, got off the motor-cycles, and parked them in the shade. I had to shake off the dust and stretch my legs. Some of the guys went ahead to the riverbank and did a mini puja—touching the water and making certain arm motions in some sort of religious way that I didn't understand. Rivers are seen as gods in India, and they were likely giving their respect to this god. We snapped a few photos, and, as always, the guys were laughing, giggling, and tus-sling with one another. While Naveen was snapping the photo, he said something in Hindi, and then Rohit swatted Ravi's groin area. Apparently, Ravi was "pitching a tent" in his jeans, and Naveen didn't want that in the photo. Their laughs were curtailed as Naveen took charge and organized us for our next activity.

Now, it was another dusty but thrilling ride back to the village. Ravi wanted me to ride with him, but Naveen still refused. The day was starting to warm up to Indian temperatures in April, that is, ninety-five degrees, and it was nice to be moving through the air again. I was happy to be out-side of Delhi's urban sprawl and to be surrounded by farmlands.

Just before we arrived at the village, Naveen motioned for us to stop at a home along the way. I didn't know where we were going, but I followed the leader. We parked the motorcycle and dusted off our jeans. Entering a compound, we found an older man sitting on a chair in a covered patio.

I noticed that as the guys greeted the man, they touched what appeared to be his lower leg. I hadn't seen or read anything about this custom, but I assumed it was a sign of respect for this older gentleman. It reminded me of the bowing rituals in other Asian societies. I wondered if the tradition had been to kiss or touch his feet, but more recently it had become acceptable to touch just above the feet.

I was introduced to this older man and offered a chair. A few kids came out of the house and became curious about me. They stayed in the background as we adults sat. The group chatted in Hindi with the gentleman, and again I tried to look interested, but really I was just taking in the surroundings and enjoying sitting in the shade. Moments later a woman came out with a tray of tea and some store-bought cookies, or biscuits, as they're called in the United Kingdom's Commonwealth of Nations. I took a biscuit and then the glass of chai, which by now I had learned was more milk than tea.

Generally I don't eat junk food, and so far I was eating all the foods that I would never have eaten normally. But there was no way of refusing. How would I explain the diet wars I had been bombarded with back home? Refuse gluten in the land of chapati? Because I couldn't explain myself to anyone who knew enough English to understand, I graciously accepted what was offered to me. Perhaps there was a lesson in there for me to relax a bit on my food choices.

The piping hot chai was served in glasses, and I had learned to hold the top of the glass because the glasses were too warm. I enjoyed the milky sweetness and taste of ginger in the tea. It was nice to be in the shade and to get a time-out from the focus being on me. Well, their discussion must have been finished, as Naveen looked to me and asked, "Peter, we will go now?" I nodded, slowly stood up, shook the host's hand, and thanked him both in English and Hindi. I waved to his wife as we left.

We got back on the motorcycles and drove just a bit farther into the village. Next up was Naveen's house. His mother held a hose and was squirting the dust and dirt off her cow with water. The cow seemed to be enjoying the attention. We went up some stairs to a bedroom that he shared with his two brothers. We sat; I enjoyed being out of the sun and not being on display in front of strangers. I enjoyed meeting their family and neighbors, but it required effort from which I needed a little break.

I looked around his room. Sparse walls that needed to be painted. A small, old black-and-white television was at the foot of the beds. I noticed a large picture of Hanuman on the wall, the monkey god who helped defeat the demon king, Ravana. I remembered learning about him in our school assembly about the Indian holiday called Dushera. I pointed to it, and Dhruv told me who it was. I learned later that this was their favorite god, or at least the god they prayed to. Hanuman was a devotee of Lord Rama, who was one of many avatars, or incarnations, of Lord Vishnu, one of the supreme gods of Hinduism. I read later that the cousins' ancestors were originally from the Afghan region, and they were brought over and groomed to be the protectors of the Indian rulers of that time. Theirs is a caste of fighters and protectors, just like the monkey god. I realized that it would make sense that the god they chose to worship was Hanuman. As the raj era is long gone, today, this caste produces India's best-known wrestlers.

Before long we were brought some chai, this time more cardamom fragrant, in small steaming glasses. Again, I held the glass from the top, as the middle was piping hot. I was starting to get hungry, but the fresh cow's milk in this tea began to satiate my hunger. I wondered how typical it was to skip lunch. These cousins, and most of the village, were not the heavyset people whom I had often seen in the wealthy classes of Delhi. Perhaps they only ate two meals a day. I was learning that milky chai was one way to hold you over until dinner.

It was decided to take a walk around the village. I walked down the stairs and saw various sari-veiled women scrubbing pots or preparing food in the courtyard below. Why wasn't I introduced to them? We stepped onto the dirt road, avoiding potholes and staying closer to the shady side of the street. We visited two more homes of people they knew and followed the same routine. I would shake hands and then politely sit while the others spoke in Hindi. I started to feel like I was an object brought to show and tell, and that was OK. This is what creating good relations between countries is all about. I might have been the only non-Indian to set foot in the village, so the least I could do was to sit there and smile and accept their biscuits and chai. In fact, I was even getting to the point where I was looking forward to the fresh milk chai.

Somehow four hours had flown by, and it was time to get back to the taxi and Mr. Singh. I was a little excited to get back. My not being in control for all those hours left me feeling a bit vulnerable and tired. The cousins wanted me to send Mr. Singh back on his own and for me to take the bus back on Sunday. I told them that I needed to get back, but they insisted I spend the night. I told them I needed to go home, and I would stay the night on another visit when I could plan better. They looked a little defeated, but they obliged my wishes.

Ravi finally got his chance, and I sat on the back of his motorcycle this time for the return trip to the main road. We seemed to be going a bit faster than before because the guys realized time was further along than they had thought. We got to the taxi car, and there was Mr. Singh waiting faithfully. I wondered what he had done all day. I knew I had chosen the right driver. I was glad to see him.

The cousins pointed to the road and at the many broken-down buses that passed their village road going into Delhi and told me that next time I should take a bus. I'm sure they were feeling bad that I had spent so much money on a taxi. I smiled and said that we would see. It felt like I had done my duty visiting the village and didn't think I would be back, but I smiled as if it were a possibility. They stood there and smiled with their oh-so-white teeth.

As we pulled away, I reflected that as much as I was enjoying the idea of heading back to Delhi, I felt I'd had a wonderful day. I had been totally distracted from all the responsibilities of my life. Besides getting out of Delhi's smog and busy lifestyle and learning a bit about village life, I had connected with five young men who had opened themselves up to me and expressed such warmth and even love for me. I was amazed at how much one can get to know another even without the ability to communicate in the same language!

But, at this point, my agenda was to return to my sanctuary, my apartment, and to only look over my balcony at India. From my apartment I could visit India on my terms, stepping out the door when I needed to buy groceries or go for a walk. That's how I wanted it to be for the time being.

Chapter Seven

While at work the following week, I thought fondly of my visit. It seemed surreal at times. Here I was having lunch with three expat teachers and wondering if they ever would have done what I did. Then I reflected on my privilege in taking such a risk: being male, having no dependents, and having served in the Peace Corps. When they asked me how my weekend was, I did share that I had been invited to a village and had an interesting experience. "How cool!" one remarked. I asked about their weekends, and all three said they had been busy with rehearsals for the faculty musical.

I remember being encouraged to try out for a part in *Into the Woods* and having a hard time declining. That's what I had done in high school, and since then I had been an avid fan of Broadway musicals. But I was in India. Why would I want to spend my time doing that when outside of the school's massive stone wall and barbed wire was the rest of the Punjab waiting to be discovered? Instead, I told the musical director that I would be too drained from a day of teaching to do the two-hour rehearsals after school.

The more days that passed after my visit to the village, the more my heart fondly remembered the experience. I reflected on how lovely it had been to spend time with them. I looked around at my students who came from many different countries and wondered if they would ever get to see India as I had seen it that Saturday. Even the few ethnically Indian students in the school, due to their economic privilege, would probably never have spent the day in a village as I had. Or maybe they had, visiting relatives perhaps, but likely on different terms. Eventually, the visit became a memory, and I was full swing into work and expat life.

But that ended. Soon, texts from the cousins from Haryana started coming again, this time asking when I was going to *spend the night* in the village. I was able to put it off for a while, stating that I had just been there and that I needed to focus on work for a while. But they were persistent, even to the point of telling me which Saturday I was coming. The unbearably hot summer was just around the corner, so I figured I had better do it immediately. How would I sleep without air conditioning?

This time I would take a train. If the Kassana cousins usually used the train to get to and from Delhi, then I could. I researched the trains online and was pleasantly surprised to see that there were several that went to their village. The Indian Railways website made it look pretty organized. I was thinking it shouldn't be so bad. After all, the British left a legacy of a large network of efficient trains that reached all the corners of India. I could do it.

Chapter Eight

On the designated Saturday morning, I left my apartment and walked to the corner taxi stand, where I took my daily taxis to work and elsewhere. The drivers there worked on a rotation schedule, and I never knew which driver I would get. I had my favorite, Arjan, a Sikh, who was younger than the others and with whom I had a great relationship. He was a gentle man, dutiful in his role as a driver. I trusted him, and he trusted me. He was not married yet and was saving money to return to his village in the Punjab to do so. He always kept himself neatly dressed, with his shirt tucked in and turban tightly wound. He had three colors of turban fabric that he rotated, depending on the shirt he wore: white, marigold, and purple.

It was his turn to take a customer, but I caught him unprepared. He had just bathed and was combing his hair in preparation for tying it above his head. I had known him for almost a year and had never seen his hair. He was always neatly coiffed on previous trips. Did he sleep in that day? He was wearing his shoes and trousers but was shirtless. That didn't surprise me. I was used to seeing the drivers sleep, eat, and bathe at this taxi stand. What shocked me was seeing Arjan's hair. It billowed to his waist! It was thick, jet black, and wavy. I reacted as if I was seeing him naked, and I'm sure I blushed. I had never seen a man with hair to his waist. Should I keep looking or turn away? His hair was always covered and now it was fully exposed. The closest image I had seen was on a poster of an Indian god, Shiva, blue skinned, large eyed, and with the same long, black hair. Arjan smiled at me and then dutifully wrapped his hair up, followed by several turns of his marigold-colored turban. I wondered if he was proud of his beautiful hair. I knew women who would have been envious of those locks!

Arjan dropped me at the station and directed me to the ticket office. That was reassuring in the chaos of the train station. I worked my way into the office and tried to determine which window to use. Much of the signage was written in Hindi, but there was enough in English for me to find the correct ticket window. This wasn't as difficult as I had thought. I secured a ticket, and it cost less than a dollar. Amazing! I reached the platform and was able to determine my train without much effort. Faridabad was the largest town before my stop, and the electronic signage present helped enormously. As the train approached the platform, I noticed passengers hanging out the door. Uh oh, the train was already full. I wondered how I would get on. There were others who wanted to get on as well, and I followed their lead. Thankfully, I didn't have any luggage except for my backpack. Somehow I was able to step on before others, and I secured a spot against a wall near the door.

The entire train was filled with Indians, not a tourist in sight. At that point, I realized I was going to be pressed against the wall for the duration of the journey. At least I had a wall to lean against. Passengers in the center of the corridor were pressed against other passengers. I looked around at the occupants of the train, and they looked at me, especially the children. I'm only five feet ten inches, but I was a head above most of the others. In the expressions of the folks around me, I saw that they were concerned for my comfort. I smiled and showed that I would be OK via some facial expressions and that, yet again, we were all in this boat together. At least I wasn't hanging off the side of the train as several other men were doing.

Just when I thought I couldn't fit even my fist between the body of the older lady in front of me and mine, a train employee somehow squeezed himself between us and repeated this throughout the corridor of the train. Perhaps he was headed to the front of the train? I couldn't believe he managed it! Later, a man selling samosas, even more amazingly, did the same thing. He squeezed his skinny body through people, all the while holding his aluminum tray of freshly fried, cumin-scented savory pastries on his hand above his head. Passengers helped balance the tray when necessary, understanding the difficulty of his work.

The train made several stops before reaching my destination. Each time, passengers pushed their way out and others pushed their way in, always leaving some travelers behind on the platform, who, while disappointed, would have to wait for the next train. Through these exchanges I got pushed farther inside the train, unfortunately away from the breeze that was keeping me from passing out from heat exhaustion. I'm sure my face was bright red from my blood trying to reach the surface to cool. Then I started to worry about being able to exit when it was my time to get down. I got off successfully but saw no sign of the Kassana cousins. I exited the small station and waited near the car park in a shady spot.

Again, the looks I received from the locals suggested I was likely the only American, who was not ethnically Indian, to get off at this stop. A smiling husband-wife couple approached me, pushing their twelve-year-old son ahead of them to greet me with his hand extended. I shook his hand, and he practiced some of the English he had learned in school. "What is your name?" "Where are you from?" and other textbook phrases were recited to me. He didn't seem so concerned about the answers, but I patiently responded in slow, clear English, so that he could be rewarded for his efforts. I am a teacher after all. They left, and then I decided to text the guys, since I didn't want to continue to be the special attraction at this railroad station anymore.

As I took out my flip phone, their dusty sedan pulled up, and I spotted the smiles behind the windshield. "Peter!" I heard Manish shout. Hugs and smiles, and then Vishnu said, "We go to cousin house, now."

"OK," I replied.

We got in the car and took off, driving off the pavement and onto a dirt road in the opposite direction of their village. We kept going, and going. I assumed the cousin was in a village close to the main road. Finally, I asked Vishnu where the cousin lived. "Rajasthan." That was the next state over, and we would be in the car another two hours. "Oh, I thought. OK." Again, I told myself to give up control and do the "when in Rome" thing.

We arrived in the bright sun of afternoon at their uncle's compound. I believe they wanted to go there because his home was a little bit nicer for me and perhaps more comfortable for sleeping than their homes. There was a large neem tree outside of the walled compound. Ravi reached up and broke a stick from a branch. He pulled off some of the bark with his fingernails and then lightly squashed the interior fibers with his teeth. Then he began to rub the soft fibers against his teeth. Dhruv approached me and said "toothbrush tree."

We entered the compound, and I met the family. His uncle stepped to the edge of the patio. He walked with a limp, and I learned later that he, like many others in this village, had had polio as a child (only recently has India been taken off the World Health Organization's polio-endemic list). There were no hugs with the greetings. Each of the Kassana cousins walked up to Uncle Raja and touched his lower calf. There was no introduction to or mention of his wife.

I met Uncle Raja's mother next. She was a heavyset woman who shook my hand with both of hers and gave a big smile, a few teeth missing. Grandma had bracelets on both hands and a gold nose stud that matched her earrings. She wore a royal-blue skirt and a long-sleeved, orange blouse. She seemed to always be busy around the house, milling about, picking up things, or cleaning, even in the middle of the night.

By the look of Uncle Raja's large, enclosed compound, I guessed he was doing well in his profession. There were two latrines off the large courtyard. Later, when I used the latrine, the cobwebs laced above the squat toilet would tell me these bathrooms weren't used very often. The house was made of cement blocks and was L-shaped. Uncle's domain seemed to be in the wing closest to the entrance; everyone else was in the back along with the kitchen.

Most excited of all was a little boy named Sanjay. He had been told I was coming and had been waiting all day for my arrival. He followed me around as the guys showed me the compound, and then he sat and stared at me. His older brother, Rohan, was about fourteen or fifteen years old and, like the others, was slender. He had remarkably beautiful grayish-green eyes. His hair was very light for an Indian. He was proof that Alexander's armies from Macedonia had come through northern India and had left some DNA behind. Rohan seemed to take on the role of the servant in the home, as I didn't see many females on this visit. We sat on the bed and snapped photos of me seated with interchanging relatives, including Grandma. After the photos, we had some chai and then set out to visit a Hindu temple. Thankfully, it was very close to this village.

Chapter Nine

It's very common for young Indian men to make a pilgrimage to nearby Hindu temples. Whereas American men would get the guys together to go fishing, watch a sporting event, or hit a bar, Indian men would make these pilgrimages. We drove through the town and found a place to park before the long line of pilgrims. Little Sanjay came with us, and he was visibly thrilled to be on the journey with his older cousins and me.

I knew we were close because I saw pilgrims walking in circles around a holy site just before the temple. Apparently this was a ritual stop pilgrims made before they reached the temple. We drove past that and went straight for the temple. We removed our shoes, and the excited Kassana cousins almost ran through the temple doors. As we entered the doorway, each reached up to swing the clapper of the brass bell that was above the entry. They signaled for me to ring the bell as well. I gave them a "why?" look, and they communicated to me that it was to let the gods know we had arrived, to wake up the gods. OK.

We proceeded up an open-air but sheltered hallway and found ourselves at a higher elevation with a few shrines to some of the gods. There were dioramas behind Plexiglas that displayed statues of a god. Marigolds and other garland-like ornaments had been draped about the statues by devotees. We continued up the hallway that took us to an even higher elevation. There was an open area with a spotless cement floor where you could pray if you wished, or you could just enjoy the shade, breeze, and view. We paused for a moment. None of our group chose to pray. They were anxious to take me farther up the hill above the temple.

Ravi took my camera and snapped photos as we approached the top of this dry, rocky, and barren hilltop. To me it looked like a good place for a crucifixion. We looked down at the temple and at the pilgrims flowing down the street. I eventually relinquished control of my digital camera, and Ravi proceeded to take several pictures of himself and his cousins—some with me, some without me, some wearing shades, and some without shades. I encouraged our leader, serious and responsible Naveen, to smile in the photos. He had such a beautiful smile, with perfect white teeth, and he shared his smile freely when he laughed, but he insisted on looking serious in photos. Some of the photos reminded me of photos of secret service agents. Later I would chuckle, as these guys were rarely serious. Eventually I did get Naveen to smile for a few photos.

The Kassana cousins were often photographed holding hands or sitting on one another's laps. It surprised me every time I saw them drape themselves over one another or hold hands—very different from American men. These young men had what was severely lacking in North America: male-male nonsexual intimacy. I had seen and experienced it in Egypt, West Africa, Europe, and now India. It was so normal and so natural to them. I noticed later in one of the photos that young Rohan had his cheek leaning against my shoulder. He was so happy to be with us, with the guys. We scampered down the hill, left the temple, and drove back to their uncle's home.

It was getting dark. Uncle Raja invited us to have a drink with him in one of the rooms. I gladly accepted and was given a chair at his table. The cousins sat on a bench to our side and instinctively refused the beer. Instead, Rohan found them some soda. Dhruv finally accepted the beer, so he drank along with Uncle Raja and me. I wondered why he was able to accept while the others were not. Perhaps since he was the eldest of the guys?

Uncle held court and did most of the talking, in Hindi. Occasionally, he'd ask the nephews to translate for him. It was evident Uncle Raja had started his drinking earlier; his glossy, dilated eyes suggested it was harder liquor. The sun had set, my belly was filled with beer, and I could smell dinner. We left their uncle and moved to the room with a huge bed. That is where we would dine and later sleep, or try to sleep, in my case.

We sat cross-legged on the bed while the food was brought out on large, round, steel platters by little Sanjay and his brother. Where were the women? While I had met the grandmother, I had been introduced to no other women. I knew that food preparation was the domain of Indian women, but I found it curious that they didn't participate in our visit, remaining in the shadows. In a Muslim family of this social standing, this would be expected. I was learning that the Rajasthani Hindus must have adopted some of these customs.

The various dishes were in metal bowls arranged around the platter. A tall stack of buttered chapati rounds were on a separate tray. Chapati is similar to tortillas but are made with whole wheat and slathered with butter. While I would have liked to have washed my hands first, I went with the flow. I was starving, and the stack of chapati was dripping with butter. I had been avoiding gluten for three years, not because I had celiac disease, but because I felt better without it. Once again, the Paleo Diet would not be observed that night.

At that moment, I was preparing to dive straight into the chapati. I watched how the others ate and tried to mimic their table manners. They tore pieces from the chapati and used each piece to grab some vegetables or lentils. Rohan would return with more chapati, fresh off the fire. I paused between mouthfuls and thought to myself that I had never tasted butter that delicious. Was it butter or was it ghee? Was it pasteurized? Was it churned that day? Although I didn't see a cow, there must have been at least one on the premises. I didn't ask any of my questions; I just enjoyed the experience.

The meal was followed by some chai, this time with cardamom predominating the flavor. Chai to me is a misnomer, as it has very little tea; it is mostly warmed, sweetened milk. I imagined the milk was likely from the same family cow that provided us with the butter.

We were all tired and practically collapsed on the king-size bed. We positioned the five of us on the bed, three heads on one side, two on the other, with our legs weaved between. They gave me the spot next to the window with a fan. I was grateful. The air from the fan blew across our clothed bodies, making sleep a definite possibility. I knew Sanjay would have liked to have stayed with us, but he had disappeared earlier; perhaps he had an earlier bedtime.

It took me a while to fall sleep, but thankfully I did. Later I awoke when the fan stopped working. Apparently the home's electricity went out. Ugh. Besides keeping us cool, the fan had kept the mosquitoes away. I calculated the fan was out for about two hours, and I dodged mosquitoes for all of those two hours. Nobody else seemed to be bothered. When the fan finally kicked on, I did fall back to sleep and was only interrupted once when Grandma turned on the light for some reason. I guess I had totaled about five hours of sleep that night. It could have been worse. Morning arrived with bright sunshine and then one by one the cousins arose from the bed.

The cousins invited me to go for a morning walk, and I motioned them to wait for me as I went to urinate in the latrine. We approached a dry field with scrub bushes, and I noticed a few folks squatting discreetly about them. The guys told me to go to the field to use the bathroom. I more or less told them to go ahead without me, as I couldn't do that on command. They did; I waited; and then we continued on our walk.

I wondered why they didn't use the latrine in the home. I had read online that half of India's population defecates outdoors, and that cell phones were more common than toilets in India. I suppose the priority of staying connected with family and friends trumped the need to properly dispose human waste.

This reminded me of a much-publicized statement from an Indian administrator in charge of preparing the Commonwealth Games in New Delhi. As was done with the World Cup and the Olympics, stadiums and housing were constructed in anticipation of the event. When the international inspectors came to check on the progress just weeks before the athletes would arrive, the inspectors were appalled at the state of the bathrooms. They were far from meeting international standards of hygiene. Dirt-caked toilets and sinks, paw prints on mattresses, sinks stained with the spittle of chewed tobacco, and soiled rooms dominated their findings. The Indian commissioner's lame explanation was something to the effect that Indians just have different standards of hygiene than foreigners. This caused a lot of ruckus in the press, with debate about "hygiene as hygiene" and having one international standard as opposed to having a standard for India and a different standard for the rest of the world.

We returned to the compound, and I was happy to be greeted with chai. Naveen, leading as usual, told me we would be bathing. We went into the backyard of the compound where there was a tap over a large cement basin, likely for washing clothes. Naveen, Ravi, Rohit, and I followed. We stripped down to our briefs. Dhruv chose to remain clothed and just observed. I tried to enquire why he wouldn't be bathing, and the cousins joked that it was because Dhruv had the largest penis. Perhaps he was shy about this and didn't want to expose himself in wet underwear? Oh well, I followed the leader and took the bucket of water handed to me and doused myself, followed by soaping myself down with a bar that Ravi handed to me. I remembered the routine from my time in Cameroon: work from the top down. Finally, I rinsed off by stepping into the basin and pouring cups of water over me.

Whereas their hands and faces always appeared to me as evenly toned brown, I could see that their bodies, which I noticed were not exposed to the sun, appeared more olive toned in their briefs. As they bathed I could see their small waists transition to relatively full buttocks. Their thick thighs tapered to thin ankles. Their shoulders were noticeably broader than their hips. Don't get me wrong; they were not built like Greek gods. They were skinny, vegetarian-fed guys from the village. However, the blueprint for physical proportionality that a Greek or Roman sculptor would use was certainly evident. I imagined that the addition of some animal protein to their diets and some light weight lifting would quickly make heads turn back home. And, of course, like Indians both north and south, they all had a full head of shiny, jet-black hair and shiny, supple skin to match. None of the beer bellies that we would see in their contemporary twenty somethings in the United States.

Expats had told me that the most beautiful Indian women were from southern India, and the most handsome men were to be found in the north. Northern Indian men had lighter skin and more angular faces. Southern Indian women tended to have softer, rounder faces. I don't think the Kassana cousins realized the assets they possessed. Perhaps they didn't need to, since their marriages were, or would be, arranged by their families.

I was the only one to have brought a fresh pair of briefs, so after drying myself with the shared, tattered towel, I removed my wet underwear and replaced them with fresh ones. The others put their pants on over the wet underwear. I supposed the dryness of arid Rajasthan would quickly take care of the soggy drawers.

Uncle Raja had a plan for me that day: he wanted to introduce me to his friends around town. He spoke no English, and I spoke no Hindi. Hmm. Somehow, we did OK. Again, I was toted around as a trophy, a conversation piece. I obliged, listened to the conversations in Hindi, smiled, and, at that point, not only did I happily accept the chai and packaged cookies offered to me but I looked forward to them. Would it taste more like ginger, cardamom, or cinnamon this time? But enough was enough with the visits. I knew it was important for him, but after three visits—one to a home, shop, and office each—I was anxious to get back to his nephews and start our return journey.

Our drive back to Haryana was uneventful, but the cousins had a ball as usual. They laughed and kidded one another for the entire three-hour country-road drive. When we got to the main road of their village, I told them I'd best be getting back to Delhi. They insisted I come into their village, but I put my foot down and said I had to get my lessons ready for the week. I told them I would not return on the train to Delhi but would rather try the bus.

They stood with me along the busy asphalt highway and waited for the right bus, one with an alert, sober-looking driver and that wasn't too full. Dhruv took charge and identified a suitable bus. It looked like a hollowed-out, all-windows-opened, tin container on wheels. He flagged it to pull over, and the guys pushed me up the first high step and told the driver my destination. As the bus pulled away, I walked toward the middle seats and bent down toward the window level to wave to my Haryana friends. I guess there was no time for good-bye hugs.

While I was happy to be heading back where I controlled my life, I knew I would miss their youthful energy and smiles. Once again, I was leaving with a warmed heart. The bus had seen better days, but at least I had a seat, all of the windows were open, creating a breeze on me, and, above all, it was headed to Delhi. I smiled from that warm and fuzzy feeling of being taken care of, being loaded onto the correct bus, and being sent off with waves and smiles. Perhaps since I was in a profession where I gave, gave, gave, and then gave a bit more, I appreciated folks giving to me, paying attention to me.

I had a flashback of when my grandfather used to clean me up after a trip to the beach at Lake Michigan. He'd lift me up onto a table on his porch, in the Rogers Park neighborhood of Chicago's North Side, and then take a towel and wipe all the sand off me. He'd get every last grain of sand, even those between my toes. That's attention that a little boy with six siblings didn't always get. I seemed to be getting that individual, doting attention again. It felt good.

As we got closer to Delhi, I asked a young man and his mother seated across from me if they could tell me where to get off if I wanted to reach my part of town, Vasant Vihar. Thankfully, the son, a university student, spoke English well and was happy to help me. His mother wanted me to come to their home in Delhi for chai sometime. After lots of pleasant conversation, we exchanged phone numbers. I knew when I took their information that I would never call them.

I had a full-time, demanding teaching job and found it difficult enough to squeeze in time with my expat friends. I told myself that I had to nurture what I had rather than start new friendships. It was so sweet to have left the warm, hospitable Kassana cousins and then moments later meet new people on a bus who were equally warm and welcoming to me. Is this how famous people go through life? Everyone seemed to want my attention.

India seemed to be populated with a billion friends I had yet to meet.

Chapter Ten

Well, it was my turn to invite the Kassana cousins to my house. I was a little nervous about that because my apartment, which was provided to me by the school, was very nice. In fact, it was much nicer than my condo back in the United States. I had purchased some local art and had something hanging on all the walls. My couch and chairs were recovered to match. The apartment was a very large, two-bedroom penthouse of a three-story building. I didn't want to flaunt the differences between my home and theirs. I'm sure the Kassanas would wonder, "Why all this for just one person?"

I remembered a time when I was working at a high school on the northwest side of Chicago. This was not a fancy magnet or restricted-enrollment school. This was a neighborhood school straddling an old, Polish-immigrant community along with a Puerto Rican and African American neighborhood. Students came from working-class homes, and most students qualified for free or reduced-price lunches.

I proposed to the principal to do a field trip/exchange with students from New Trier, the suburban high that I had attended. I thought it would be a great idea for the students to meet one another and gain some understanding of one another's worlds. My principal was a seasoned administrator and an intelligent, caring man. He had made great strides in his tenure there, turning a school that previously didn't hold assemblies due to inappropriate student behavior to one that had several assemblies with properly behaving students.

He knew better than me, a fresh-out-of-college idealist. He told me that my intentions were good, but that our city kids would get the shorter end of the stick with such an exchange. He went on to explain that the New Trier kids would come back with a better appreciation of their privilege, but the city kids would come back realizing what they didn't have. He didn't think that would be fair to his students and therefore wisely denied my request.

Twenty years later, here I was again in a similar situation. I wasn't sure if my Haryana friends realized what a different world I lived in. Would they think differently of me after seeing my apartment? I told myself that this was who I was and how I lived, and I really did want to have them over to reciprocate their hospitality and kindness and to give them the opportunity to get to know me better. Come what may, I decided to do it. I told them they could come on a Saturday and spend the night. At least that would give me Friday to rest from the school week.

Chapter Eleven

In anticipation of their visit, I told the woman I hired to cook and clean for me, Mrs. Kaur, to prepare only vegetarian dishes and perhaps some rice that I could reheat for them. Mrs. Kaur came on Saturday morning and cooked her Punjabi specialties: *shahi paneer* (cubes of fresh cheese in a "royal" style tomato-minced onion sauce), *saag* (creamed spinach), *dal makhani* (buttered and stewed brown lentils), and basmati rice. Perfect. They were my favorites too. The Kassana cousins would be pleased.

She left around noon, her normal Saturday time, but asked if I wanted her to stay and help with their visit. I thanked her but declined her offer and told her that I would be fine.

I expected the cousins to arrive around two that afternoon from the old Delhi train station, but I didn't see them until about four thirty. From the train station in downtown Delhi, they took a bus as far as they could, but buses only went so far and didn't reach neighborhoods like mine. Vasant Vihar was filled with many expats renting the investment homes of retired Indian military officers. The guys didn't want to pay for a taxi, so they walked the rest of the way.

Kumar, the Nepalese man who served in the Indian Army troop of my landlord and who worked as the guard of his home, escorted them up the three flights to my door. He looked at me protectively, and I immediately thanked him and assured him that these were indeed my invited guests.

The guys entered, sweaty but happy. They instinctively removed their shoes and hugged me. All of them took a look around my place, not hiding their surprise. They seemed very happy—large, spacious, sunny, a computer, Wi-Fi, two bedrooms, a separate dining room, oriental rugs, well appointed, and a large outdoor patio where I had a small plant container garden. I told them I had beer in the refrigerator if they would like. First they refused, but then Naveen decided to have a beer. Quickly the others followed suit. They seemed surprised and outwardly happy to have such a supply of beer in the fridge.

After relaxing and chatting and laughing, I asked them if they were ready to eat. They were, and I took them to the kitchen to see what was prepared. The guys lifted up the pots and started speaking to one another in Hindi. I wondered what the issue was, and I asked if there was a problem. They asked if there was chapati. I replied that I didn't have chapati, but that Mrs. Kaur had made rice for us. They conferred with one another again and then looked back at me and said, "No chapati?" I again told them I had no chapati, but that I had rice and hoped that would be OK. After all, I had been to Indian restaurants in Chicago my entire adult life and never once saw chapati, only rice and naan, a pita bread baked with white flour. I then motioned to them to take a bowl and begin serving themselves.

They again huddled, spoke in Hindi, and looked toward me and asked if I had any flour. I told them that, unfortunately, I didn't have any flour in the house. They asked if there was a place nearby where they could purchase flour. I told them there was a dry goods shop around the corner, but I tried one last time to offer the prepared rice. Naveen told me that Ravi and Rohit were going to go buy some flour and that they would make chapati. I was a little bit surprised. After all, who doesn't like rice? They were guests at my home and, as much as I went with the flow in their village, they were unwilling to substitute rice for their starch. I didn't show my disappointment and instead offered Naveen and Dhruv another beer. We chatted away until the guys returned with the flour.

The magic started when they proceeded to create chapati with whole wheat flour, some water, and a little salt. They used the side of the beer bottle to roll them into round, flat pieces of dough. Working together, they laid each on the gas flame and flipped them just before they were charred. Like an assembly line, in no time they had a tower of chapati, buttered and resting on a clean napkin. While sipping my beer, I watched the whole event with awe. From the buttery scent that pervaded my kitchen, I knew

I would enjoy their creation. We moved the party to my living room and feasted at my coffee table.

I never understood exactly why they insisted on chapati and not rice. I didn't feel comfortable questioning them about this since it was such a big deal to them. I wondered if they had ever eaten a meal without chapati.

After we ate, Naveen asked if he could use my laptop. He wanted to check his e-mail and do some web surfing. Their village didn't have Internet access, so when they wanted to work on a computer, they would have to go to the main road and use an Internet café. Naveen looked content, lying on the bed with a laptop. He wanted a photo taken of him doing so, and then the others followed suit.

It was past my bedtime. As a teacher, my eyes, even on the weekend, rarely stayed open past ten o'clock. I was nervous about how I would handle the sleeping arrangements. Should I invite one or two of the four to join me in my queen bed and let the others stay in the spare bedroom? How would I decide who sleeps where?

I'm used to sleeping alone and knew I wouldn't sleep as well with another in my bed. I was exhausted from the school week and had another full teaching week ahead. They probably would want to be together anyway, so I told them I would sleep alone and was going to turn in early. I imagine Naveen, the leader, slept in the twin bed and the other three slept in the queen bed.

I could hear belly laughter from the spare room as I fell asleep. These guys had fun until the last minute of the day! It felt strange to be sleeping apart from them, but I didn't know any other way to do it, and in the end, they were completely fine, and I actually slept.

The next morning they showed me how to make chai. It was a more complicated procedure than I thought. First, you boil water. Then you break two cardamom seeds above the water and drop the green shells in with the black seeds. Add the fresh ginger and then the sugar. Then the black tea gets spooned into the pot. Last, in goes the cold milk that stops the boil. Just after the now thick and milky mixture returns to a boil, you turn off the heat. Pour it through a strainer into each cup to keep the tea and spice shells behind. Delicious!

There was some news I had to break to them before they left my apartment for the train. I had decided not to renew my contract with the school and to return to the States. My parents were aging, my nieces and nephews were school age, and I wanted them to know me better. I loved India, but the streets of Delhi were getting more and more crowded, making driving mostly a matter of sitting in traffic. Most disturbing was that the air quality in Delhi was deteriorating by the day. I was enjoying my job and enjoying experiencing India, but the Delhi situation was one I was choosing to leave. If only they could move the school to rural Haryana, where the air was cleaner!

The Kassana cousins were disappointed upon hearing the news. I told them that we would keep in touch. They insisted on my making one more overnight visit to their village. As much as I wanted to do our good-byes at the time, I had to agree to another trip. We were closer now, and I wanted to part with some appropriate closure. Normally my weekends were about recovering from the exhausting work week. I needed my space to decompress and reenergize for the next school week. Like many teachers, I was territorial about how I spent my precious weekends. I could do a Haryana trip one more time. I knew that after every visit to their village, I came back feeling warm and fuzzy and better educated about India.

Of course, I would make one more trip before I left India in June.

Chapter Twelve

A month later, Naveen texted me with a proposed plan to meet on a week-end when a wedding was planned. He wanted me to join them as their guest. I agreed, this time planning on taking the local bus to and from Haryana. While so much of India can seem chaotic and messy, the Delhi metro was spotless and organized. I took it to the end of the line, where it shared a terminal for buses heading to the states south of Delhi. I was successful in finding the buses to Haryana. I entered a bus, took a seat near a window, and waited for it to fill up.

The journey began and we traveled for about forty-five minutes, when the bus pulled over at a busy intersection. We were in Faridabad. Apparently this was the last stop of this bus, and I had to change buses to reach the Kassanas' village. I said the name of the village to the non-English-speaking ticket collector, and he took my arm and walked me off the bus and along the road past a few more buses. He walked me about a block away into a new bus. He sat me down and said something to the driver in Hindi. I arrived in the village thirty minutes later, and the guys were waiting in Rohit's dusty sedan.

We did our greetings and hugs, and I took a better note of them this time. Naveen and Dhruv would each give me a quick hug. Ravi would wrap his arms around my waist, and when he would let go, he would mur-mur "Oh Peter." Rohit, being the shortest, would lean his head against my chest as he hugged me.

Naveen and Dhruv were anxious for me to open the backseat door of the sedan. I sensed there was a joke involved. I could hear restrained giggles as I opened the back door. I peered in and the cause of their laughter became apparent. The backseat footwells were filled with chaffs of sugarcane. Apparently, on their way to the bus stop, they had stopped at the side of the road and cut stalks of sugarcane from a farm. Rohit, who was driving, asked them to be sure to spit the bark of the cane out the window to prevent messing up his car. Of course the guys did the opposite, spitting the bark onto the floor of Rohit's car. There were about two inches of cane bark on the footwells and beyond. The guys were splitting their sides laughing because Rohit was upset at their messing up his family's car.

Up to that point, I hadn't been to the homes of Ravi, Manish, or Rohit. This being our fourth weekend together, they knew me much better and wanted their families, including the female members, to know me. We visited each family's home in succession and took our "last" photos at all venues—lots of smiles, listening to them talk about me in Hindi, and delicious chai and store-bought biscuits.

Whereas most of the females in the homes I had visited in the past had been more reclusive, that day it was different. I hadn't recollected anything about the women on previous visits, except wondering why they semidraped their saris over their heads. They were not Muslim women. When I had asked Chaya at school, she had told me that the Muslims had had some influence of modesty on the local Hindu women in the north. While not a rule in the Hindu religion, it became somewhat customary in the Punjab for women to cover their hair when a male guest was at home. For this visit, word must've gone out that I was family, as I was greeted by all of their mothers and sisters. That made me happy. Women had been strangely absent on previous visits, and I had feared I was getting just the male perspective of India.

Manish had prepped his family that I would be visiting. He had a nicely whitewashed compound and two black cows and a calf next to the side of his house within the compound. We had tea and cookies in what looked to be their rarely used living room, and I offered to snap photos for them. We did many group shots, and I invited his mother to get in one. She looked excited about the opportunity and dashed inside to change her outfit. When she returned, she stepped right in. I told Manish that I thought we should have a photo of just his parents. He agreed, but I learned that it wasn't a common practice to photograph husbands with wives in this stratum of society. His mother was smiling under her bright, gold-trimmed orange veil and matching sari, while her husband looked uncomfortable and out of place. I started to wonder if I had crossed a cultural line by putting males and females together in a picture. The photo came out as awkward as possible, but I'm glad I made an effort to include the women, and I'm sure Manish's mother appreciated having a photo of herself looking so well. As we were saying our good-byes, Manish had one more request of me: "Peter, please, take picture of my cows?"

"Of course," was my response. How cute that he felt his cows were important enough for a photo!

We visited Naveen's house next. Naveen's mother and I had met before, and she greeted me that day with more familiarity. However, she seemed a little preoccupied, having just milked her cow and looking as if she had more chores to do. I could see some milk spattered on her shirt. Both Ravi and Naveen's fathers were away, serving in the Indian Army. It was the first time I realized that they must have had the responsibility of assuming the roles of the men in their homes.

Rohit's home was at the edge of town and as such would probably have been identified as a farm home rather than a town home. I met his parents and his older brother but didn't meet his wife or Rohit's wife. I learned that Rohit was married at age fifteen. He seemed a little embarrassed by this. Rohit was the third Indian I had met who had married at such a young age. For some reason I had thought that this custom would have died out, but it seemed to be more commonplace than I had imagined. Chai followed, and then the photos with family members began, each taking turns snapping photos with me. I felt like a politician with random children being placed next to me on the couch for the shoot.

Before heading to the wedding, we walked to a guava tree beyond Rohit's home, and Manish climbed it and began to toss us each a guava fruit. I rubbed it on my shirt to get the dust off and took a bite, knowing from experience to be careful while chewing the hard seeds, as you could easily lose a filling. They were as crunchy, delicious, and refreshing as I had remembered from my time in Cameroon.

We got into the car, and the laughter continued for the entire journey. Do they ever run out of steam? I had no idea what they were joking about, but I enjoyed that they were enjoying. When they weren't laughing, they spoke in Hindi, which offered me some quiet time to be able to go off into my thoughts while watching the passing Haryana countryside. We were far from any town. Yellow fields of blooming mustard greens were swaying in the organized fields. Yet again, we were traveling on a bumpy country road, which made me wonder if Rohit was avoiding the authorities on the main roads for some reason. Did he even have a license? It didn't matter; I was with happy young men who loved having me with them. I was on an adventure and far from the troubles and concerns of my work life.

While I had assumed the wedding was just down the road, this ended up being another long journey—more than two hours away. Naveen didn't tell me this when he invited me. Were we still in Haryana? As before, there was nothing I could do, so I relinquished control and sat back. They continued their conversation and laughter. I happily went back to a zoned-out state. I watched the sun set over the fields and then the gradual appearance of the stars in the sky.

I didn't know what to expect when we arrived at the wedding. Was I dressed well enough in jeans and a button-down shirt? It turned out that this was not a fancy wedding but rather more like an outdoor buffet in a community center; one and all could pop in. The Kassana cousins bumped into people they knew, one of whom spoke English pretty well. They stuck him with me. His looks were, to me, worth a second take. Stuck in a remote village, did this twenty-three-year-old know he had movie-star good looks? Back home, he would likely have had a woman by his side, but here in India, marriages were arranged, so a guy like this would be hanging with his friends rather than dating and being adored by women.

He spoke to me as Naveen and Ravi pulled some chairs together for us to sit and eat. At one point, Ravi reached over and fed me a piece of chapati. "Open your mouth, Peter!" he said, causing fits of laughter among the cousins. Rohit and Dhruv brought food to us on paper plates, and we all took a bite of whatever appeared in front of us.

Indian food never disappointed me, although getting Delhi belly was always a worry. Everyone gets "the runs" on their first week in India. On this occasion, I, once again, didn't wash my hands before eating this handheld food nor did any of the guys. Now, the fun was their reaching over to hand feed me pieces of chapati. Thankfully, it had no repercussions. Maybe this meant I was building an iron gut. Did this mean I would be capable of eating the Delhi street food I had been avoiding?

The bride and groom did make an appearance, and I was able to meet them briefly. While the wedding was not an especially formal affair, it was well attended, and everyone seemed to be having a good time. It was late. As we set off for the trip back to the Kassana cousins' village, it was pitch dark except for the brilliance of the stars in the sky.

When we reached Naveen's house, all were tired, and we went straight to his room. There were four beds, one for each of us; Ravi walked back to his home. The beds were wood framed with no mattress, just twine threaded to and from each edge, creating a hammock. The woven hammock was covered with a rug made from scrap fabric. Each bed had a blanket or two to keep us warm. I slept like a baby in the cool night air and the comfort of the cousins nearby.

We woke to the sound of cows mooing, likely aching to be milked. Soon we were brought warm ginger chai served in short glasses. Mornings in the village were cold. I pondered on how amazing it was that the milk in the tea had most likely been inside the cow an hour earlier. It hit the spot. We took a walk around town and into the field for their morning ritual before they took me back to the main road for my trip home. This was our good-bye for good, as I didn't know if or when I would see them again.

Chapter Thirteen

My friendship with locals wasn't limited to the Haryana cousins. At an expat party, I was introduced to a colleague's friend named Krishan. My conversation with Krishan was very different from those I had with my friends from Haryana. He spoke English! Krishan had an objectivity and sophistication to his thoughts about his culture. He also had a nice group of expat friends from the United Kingdom, which must have allowed him to see India from their perspective. He had many opinions, commendations, and criticisms about all things Indian and was happy to share them. He was as interested in learning about my experiences in the United States as I was in learning about his India.

Krishan was obviously used to expats and was eager to befriend and learn from them. He offered to show me around Delhi, and I gladly accepted. In return, I would invite Krishan to my home for dinner, where he could enjoy wine and meat, things he couldn't have in his home with his religious parents. Krishan had stepped away from Hinduism and therefore had no qualms about eating meat. Mrs. Kaur prepared chicken dishes for me despite being a vegetarian herself. She refused to cook beef, which I respected. Occasionally I would purchase ground bison from the US embassy commissary and prepare meatloaf myself.

Krishan's parents were devout Hindus—Brahmins in fact—members of the highest caste. His father taught English in a local college. Both of his parents were politically progressive. Krishan was fortunate to visit a friend in Europe. Upon his return, he enthusiastically recounted everything he did and saw to his parents. He told them he even ate a hamburger in Paris, and that it was delicious. With that announcement, his parents were stunned; they didn't speak to him for three weeks.

Krishan asked if I'd like to join him on a trip to his village in the Punjab to attend his cousin's wedding. By this time I had been to the Haryana village three times and felt like a seasoned pro. I loved the idea of going with Krishan because he had an acute perspective on his own culture, he spoke English very well, and he had opinions that he freely shared with me. Krishan arranged the train tickets, and we were off on a Saturday morning. Krishan secured us two seats on the air-conditioned second-class train. There was even tea-and-biscuit service. I was looking forward to the trip, as I had never traveled north on the train.

Unfortunately, one of the first views out the window was an open field in which many locals were doing their morning routine. By now I was no longer appalled by such sights. To know and to love India was to know all of her realities. Even the tourists heading to the Taj Mahal on the executive, first-class train would had to have passed this field.

Unlike my previous train experience, this train ride was pleasant because I was seated in comfort next to a great guy who was about to share his village with me. If I had a question about something I saw, I could just turn to Krishan and ask. We were headed north, crossing the border from Delhi into today's official state of Punjab.

After about four hours on the train, we got off in what looked like a small, dusty town. We collected ourselves and walked two blocks to the street with the buses. Krishan looked for the one we needed and flagged it down. The destinations were written by hand, in Hindi, on the windshields of the buses. I would never have been able to do this on my own.

The bus we entered was crowded. We squeezed through others in the aisle and found a spot to stand, where we could each hold onto the back of a seat. Curious eyes of fellow passengers were on me, but always in a polite way. Only the children stared. We were only on it for thirty minutes before we stepped off this bus to enter another. The second bus dropped us on the side of a road that led to his hamlet. The sun was strong, and I was ready for a siesta.

We crossed the street and followed a dirt road that narrowed into a lane that led into the village. On one side of the road were neatly arranged cow-dung patties drying in the sun. These were an important fuel source for the villagers and were created by mixing cow dung with hay and shaping it into rounds. The circular shape allowed it to be easily placed below their cooking pots. While in Haryana the discs were flat, more Frisbee like, here they looked more like round loaves of bread.

I started to understand why cows were sacred in India. They helped till the soil, they provided unlimited milk, ghee, cheese, and yogurt, and they even provided fuel for the fire! It makes total sense. No wonder nobody killed or ate them!

Krishan's village was different from the Haryana village. It felt like I was walking into a medieval town, as the lane was hugged by walls on both sides. The walls varied from mud to brick to cement. Breaking the continuity were the occasional door fronts. I appreciated the shade that the walls provided. Krishan's door was not far down the lane. He unlocked the door, we stepped in, and we removed our shoes. There was a small, sun-filled courtyard with a water pump which had an overly large, curved handle on top. That's where we would get our bathing water for our bucket baths that weekend. Krishan's parents didn't live there at the time; they lived with Krishan in an apartment in Delhi. Krishan and his two married sisters had access to the village home when they wanted to visit.

Krishan tidied up a bit, opening some curtains and doors to air out the place. I plopped on the bed for some quick rest, before we headed out to make the local, obligatory rounds. I was down for about thirty minutes when Krishan suggested we move on. Our first stop was to the family where we would be having our meals. As there were no restaurants in the village, and no food in the house, Krishan had made arrangements to eat with close family friends, just down the lane.

The family had two lovely daughters, twelve and sixteen years old, and an adorable son who was around six years old. All had the beautiful, large, protruding eyes that are emphasized in ancient Indian art and in representation of the gods. The father and the older sister spoke some

English, which was such a treat for me! Now, I could actually participate in the conversations. They could get a sense of who I was, and I didn't have to sit there like a smiling potted plant, as I had done in the Haryana homes.

I asked the eldest daughter about her math curriculum, since that was the subject I taught middle-school students in Delhi. She presented her book to me, and while it was written in Hindi, I could make out the problems from the diagrams. Math and music were indeed universal languages.

We didn't stay long because we knew we'd be back for dinner at sundown. Krishan just wanted to touch base with them. I liked this family, and they were amazingly hospitable people. I looked forward to returning later.

When we left their home, Krishan explained to me the unfortunate nationwide problem of female infanticide in India. He said he could point to all the homes in his village where a female fetus had been aborted, despite the practice being illegal in all of India. I had known of the statistics of this practice in India and China, but with him I could see it at a more personal level. Abortion isn't illegal, but testing for the sex of the child is. He estimated that about every other home in this village had parents who had aborted their female child to get a male child. I guessed that everyone really did know everyone else's business in a small town. Krishan didn't mention this in a gossipy way but more in an academic sense. He clearly loved his village, but he had also stepped away and was able to look at it with an objective perspective. The family whose home we had just left was to be commended because the parents actually kept their first two females. But he did say that they had aborted the third pregnancy because the baby was female, and they really did want a male child. To their credit, at least they kept the first two females.

Krishan explained how many families would see daughters as an economic burden because a daughter would require a large dowry when she married. When women marry in India, they leave their family and move into their husband's family home. In a way, the dowry is the inheritance she would have gotten when her parents died. She takes it to her new family knowing she will get nothing from her parents at the time of their deaths. I learned that a newly married woman would suffer from poor treatment from her in-laws in her husband's home until she produced a male child. After that, she would be accepted into the family. The pressure from the in-laws on the new wife to produce a male child was high, and I started to understand why abortion could be so commonplace.

The next stop was to visit a cousin of Krishan's who lived two doors down. He had a large compound. While Krishan's family's home felt more crowded among other homes, this house felt more like an expansive country home. The house was set back from the entrance with a large courtyard. I wondered if the walls were to keep the cows on their properties.

This cousin had a guest for the week, a sadhu/guru of sorts, who was giving classes or sessions to local devotees. The devotees allegedly fasted for the week and spent the days chanting slokas in this home. This was the source of the chanting I had heard before my nap. The guru wore marigold-colored robes and a bright orange turban, and he had a long white beard and a big belly and carried a cell phone. I shook the guru's hand, but Krishan did the formalities of touching his feet. Later Krishan would tell me he thought the man was a charlatan, taking money from poor villagers. Krishan didn't respect that. Krishan declined the offer of chai, stating that we had more stops. He would see his cousin later at the wedding.

Before we left that home, Krishan made a point to greet a woman who was seated on the dirt yard, away from the house, washing dishes. Krishan touched her shoulder and had some conversation in Punjabi. I watched their interaction and saw how respectful and reverential he was with this woman, who was squatting on the ground with a stack of dishes in front of her. He touched her shoulder again as he left her, and we were back on the street. As we strolled, he told me she was from the former "untouchable" caste, now called the Dalit caste. Krishan, who supported the equality of all Indians, always made a point to touch and acknowledge her on his visits. It was a political act and one of the many things I appreciated about Krishan.

On the way back to his home, we passed a group of women in front of a store with baskets. Krishan saw my inquisitive look and told me they were there to grind their wheat grains for that night's chapati. The community shared the mill, and that way all of the families benefited. I briefly wondered about how the mill was paid for, but then my thoughts changed to just appreciating the social idea of everyone sharing a resource, patiently waiting their turn, and likely catching up on the village news. Freshly ground wheat used in each meal? Wow! Is that what made the chapati so delicious? I could see why my routine of cooking once and eating "leftovers" for the rest of the week was unacceptable here. Freshly prepared meals matter in India.

We headed back to Krishan's home and prepared for some visitors who he had invited to stop by before dinner. His friends, Sandeep and Arjun, arrived and sat down with us in the courtyard around a tray of snacks we had put together from the travel munchies we had brought from Delhi. I opened a bottle of wine that I had brought, and Krishan opened a tall, cold Kingfisher beer he had purchased from the drugstore on our way home. The two young men were pleased to be joining us, and I was happy to be off the street and not being stared at for the time being.

Sandeep was also of the Dalit caste. Krishan made a point to befriend folks from the Dalit caste and was conscientiously making a political statement by inviting them to his home. Sandeep was clearly a likable, friendly person, and I was happy he came. I was wishing his English was better, but Krishan did a good job of translating when necessary.

Krishan recalled his grandmother shouting at untouchables when they'd come to her door. He was pointing at the very door of his home. He said she was terrible. She would scold them and dare them to put their filthy feet in her home. Krishan told me India had come a long way since those days; however, he also shared that there was still some lingering prejudice. India was the first country to create affirmative action legislation, initiated by Gandhi right after independence. It allowed the Dalits to get hiring preferences for government jobs. I had just assumed that affirmative action was an American-created program. India had started it twenty years earlier. It made me realize how truly great Gandhi was.

Krishan's family was part of the highest caste called Brahmins. This did not mean they were from a wealthy caste but that they did get the highest respect among all the castes. Theirs was the ancient caste of priests. They were known for their high levels of literacy and education. I was invited to an Indian party in Delhi, and the hostess wanted to make a blessing or toast of sorts, and she called out, "Is there a Brahmin in the room to do the blessing? Where's our nearest Brahmin?" She got the giggles and continued, "Where's a good Brahmin when you need one?" She was joking, of course, but I got a sense that it was a kickback to how things might have been done in the past.

The best place to get a sense of the role of Brahmins is in the sacred town of Varanasi. Tourists hire boats to watch the morning puja rituals along the banks of the Ganges. In the evenings, tourists again travel up and down the river to watch the evening rituals. After the sun sets, all the boats gather at one of the ghats so that their passengers can watch the Brahmins perform a ceremony. There are five platforms with altars, and the Brahmin priests do various rituals. There are candles, rings of fire, lots of bell ringing, chanting, and other theatrics.

Since Krishan's parents were products of the liberal sixties, they dropped their posh surname and adopted a neutral one, thus giving up the privilege that their surname bestowed on them in an effort to help the underclasses by supporting the termination of the caste system. Krishan, however, chose to keep his posh surname and had enjoyed the privilege it had given him for thirty-six years. I didn't ask him why he didn't change his surname. Krishan was human, a good person, and living in a different India than his parents did. I had already seen his acts of kindness, charity, and political conviction. His surname would probably open doors that could help him in his future.

Sandeep and Arjun seemed to have enjoyed their time with us. I wondered how often they had the opportunity to drink alcohol. Sandeep told us he would return in the morning to see us off. I was glad because I saw the goodness in him that Krishan did.

The sun was setting, and we were hungry, so we headed down to the family's home for dinner. The daughters had set up the dinner arrangements on the unfinished rooftop, where we would eat under the stars and in the breezes of the cooling night. The father ate with Krishan and me, and I relished the chance to eat freshly ground chapati with that oh-so-yummy freshly churned butter on top again. Yum, I liked how villagers ate! The rest of the vegetarian meal was equally delicious, as was the after-dinner chai. It was so quiet on the rooftop; I imagined that all of the families in the village were eating indoors at that time. And, of course, the stars were in their full glory above.

Then Krishan and I had to return to his place to get our suits and ties on for the wedding. As we got dressed, we had yet more visitors, one of whom was a good friend of Krishan's named Balbir. Balbir worked as an English teacher at a local government school. Like me, he worked a job that required a lot of energy and focus. I imagined he was paid very little. From his interest in our conversation, I got the impression that he would have liked to have spent more time learning from me. I wondered if he felt like his wings had been clipped by living in a village. I invited him to visit me in Delhi, but he never did. I would have enjoyed a visit from him. He had the qualities I appreciated of someone raised in a village coupled with the sophistication of a professional.

Since we had our suits on and the photos had been taken, it was time to head to the wedding. As we stepped onto the street, we were met by a wedding parade—not the parade of the one we would be attending but of another wedding in the village. Possible wedding dates were set by the Hindu priests according to the alignment of the stars, planets, and moon. This caused a spate of weddings to occur on the same day. A couple wouldn't dare to marry on an inauspicious day, as it might spoil their chances of a happy life together. The parade was led by three men wearing red velvet marching band costumes. Completing their uniform were matching hats. Two men were playing trumpets and the third was playing a snare drum. Behind him followed the father of the groom. He was wearing a beautiful gray suit and a turban that was a beautiful shade of bright pink. The pink turban fabric was wrapped several times around his head and, instead of being tucked into a fold, it trailed down to his waist. It really stood out against the gray, dusty walls of the lane. We waited for them and the parade of children and other guests to pass. When they passed, we unlocked Krishan's motorcycle, lifted it out of the courtyard onto the lane, bid farewell to our visitors, and headed off to town.

Sitting behind Krishan on his motorcycle, I used the opportunity to have a few laughs alone with him before we had to be on stage again. As a passenger on his motorcycle, I kept my head behind his to block the wind, but this also allowed me to speak into his left ear. I was enjoying the freedom and exhilaration of riding a motorcycle despite the risk. I gave Krishan a strong hug with an extra squeeze to thank him for this wonderful moment. I appreciated his friendship. What a gift he was giving me: the chance to meet the folks in his world and for me to ask questions about the culture where I was a guest. I loved my trips to Haryana, but I left with so many unanswered questions about the cultural aspects that I was experiencing. Those were trips that touched my heart. This was also a trip that touched my heart but it also expanded my understanding.

We found Krishan's cousin's wedding procession in full swing in town. The trumpets and drums were blaring. His cousin was seated atop a horse that was decorated from head to tail. Looking up at his cousin, I could see that he was wearing a gray suit with a red tie and had the same type of bright pink turban on his head like the one I had just witnessed. His face was handsome: a square jaw, pink, full lips, a brown complexion, a strong brow, a five o'clock shadow, and a beautiful smile. Krishan told me he had a good job with an international business in Delhi. His cousin chose his wife rather than having it arranged—a privilege of his caste and economic situation.

Krishan and I worked our way up to the horse and greeted his cousin, who reached down from his perch to shake my hand. Quickly we stepped back and joined the crowd. Krishan told me we had done our duty there and suggested we go ahead to the reception. We mounted his motorcycle and were off.

We arrived at the hall, which was just outside of town and surrounded by a field. Our approach reminded me of the barn dances I had attended during my college years in Iowa. In front of me were stars, stillness, and a hall spraying light from its doors and windows. Many guests had arrived already and were awaiting the formal arrival of the bride and groom. Krishan and I popped into the hall but quickly stepped back outside. I asked Krishan why he wasn't greeting people in the hall. He said these cousins were not close to his family. His parents had had a falling out with them—hence his parents' absence from this wedding. Wedding rituals required Krishan's family to participate. Krishan didn't seem to have any issue with the groom; his greeting had seemed warm a few moments before. Krishan and his two sisters would be representing his family despite their parents' absence.

His two sisters had just arrived and were approaching us with their families. He introduced me to them, and they were very kind. I was disappointed to learn that they didn't speak English, as I felt I would likely have found them as interesting as their brother. His sisters looked stunning. One of the reasons I enjoyed attending special occasions in India was because I got to see Indian women dressed "to the nines." That is, women of means actually wrapped in probably nine yards of gorgeous, brightly colored, often silk, fabric around them. They ended up carrying much of it draped over one arm or shoulder. It was a regal look, and his sisters looked like royalty.

The bride had arrived and was standing under a handheld canopy alongside her bridesmaids. Brides don't wear white; they wear a deep garnet red and are ornamented with gold and silver rings, bracelets, nose rings, and several other pieces of jewelry. I imagined getting her ready was like several people decorating a Christmas tree. The bride isn't smiling; rather, she looks afraid. I learned that it is customary and expected for the bride not to express too much joy or excitement at the wedding, as it would bring bad luck to the marriage. I was learning that Indians had many superstitions.

Next, the groom arrived on the horse. This time his face was veiled by the beaded ribbons hanging from his headdress. Additionally, he had a suit of ten-rupee notes pasted to a cardboard hanging from his neck. It covered the entire front of his suit like a coat of armor. With a closer look, I could see that the notes were carefully placed geometrically. Some notes were folded to create the illusion of flowers from a distance. I never asked Krishan about the meaning of the suit of rupee notes, but I expected it was another superstition to encourage financial well-being during the marriage.

Before entering the hall, the bride and groom, along with their families, performed rituals such as exchanging garlands and one family presenting the other with blankets or other gifts. Krishan and his sisters had a role in it, representing his cousin's extended family. Once those formalities were over, the bride and groom entered the hall together and took their seat on two large chairs on the stage. They remained there for what seemed like the entire night. The guests took turns standing beside them for photos. Then, a line of guests was formed and each guest stood behind the seated bride and groom waving rupee notes over their head, in front of their faces, and finally dropping them on their laps. Was this in lieu of gifts? I never asked; I just followed Krishan's lead.

Afterward, Krishan and I headed for the buffet table. The guests seemed as famished as we were. You couldn't be shy about stepping up to the food tables; otherwise others would step right in front of you. Krishan and I were able to get our fill, but it wasn't relaxing and felt like you had to elbow your way into the line. What I found surprising was that when the guests finished eating, they dropped their paper plates and utensils on the dirt floor. I did see trashcans, and I wondered why they didn't use them. We dropped our plates on the floors as well. Oh well, when in Rome.

The DJ was spinning discs by then, and I was willing to dance. It was only men on the dance floor. They, of course, were delighted to have me dancing to their music. The groom finally moved from his chair at the beckoning of the men on the dance floor. He, alone, joined us for a dance or two, but then returned to his chair. People danced to some Western tunes, but the crowd came alive when a Bollywood hit was played. The difference in exuberance was like night and day. Indians *love* their music and especially appreciate it when foreigners share it with them. The joy in their faces radiated as they mouthed the words to their songs.

The way Indians danced reminded me of how Egyptian men danced: lots of torso shaking with arms outstretched above their heads, often stretching a scarf or belt. One man even danced with a loaded rifle above his head. I didn't really understand that and was a little relieved to get off the dance floor unscathed. I did hear him firing shots outdoors later. Perhaps it was part of the celebration? Krishan was ready to leave, and I was tired, so we did.

The next morning we had breakfast at the same family's home. The menu included buttered chapati, pickled onions, and warm, milky chai. At this point, I was sold on the idea of fresh milk and was ready to bring a cow back to Delhi! I guess I couldn't complain. In Delhi, people often buy their dairy products twice a day. Almost on every corner is a dairy store kiosk. Families send their children to buy fresh milk or cheese in the morning for their next meal. The kiosks close in the afternoon and are re-stocked soon thereafter. Families make a second trip in the afternoon for the evening meal. Again, freshness matters in Indian cuisine.

I had to convince Mrs. Kaur to make a big pot of something from which I'd eat all week. That would be unheard of in an Indian home. The Indian women who worked at my school told me they would wake up an hour earlier to prepare their husband's fresh lunch to be brought to their work in stacked, metal tiffin containers. Then, they'd prepare another fresh meal for dinner. It was just not the custom to use leftovers for future meals when fresh was possible. Maybe that's why I rarely had a bad-tasting meal in India.

Krishan wanted to take me on one more stroll through the village before we set off for our return journey to Delhi. We stopped at the temple where his family worshipped. It was a plain, one-story structure with a large yard and covered walkway leading to the shrines. We left our dusty shoes on the steps and approached the three different shrines, each a representation of a different god. The usual offerings adorned the figures: fresh flower garlands (mostly marigold blooms), synthetic garlands, fruits, and even sparkly scarves draped over their bodies. Krishan told me his father took a lot of responsibility for the upkeep of the temple. The floors looked like they were washed daily, and the yard appeared equally well kept. I appreciated the shade and cross breezes it had. This seemed like a nice sanctuary to visit after a long day of working in the sun.

We continued around the edge of the village, where the farming began. Krishan had one more schoolmate to visit who was involved with farming. We sat in his yard and enjoyed another cup of chai. He didn't speak English, so I sat back in my chair and looked out at the bucolic surroundings. There was a very large, what I would call "antique," pull cart on the edge of his farm. The wheels were large and entirely made of wood—even the spokes. A horse was at the helm grazing on the grass at the side of the road. It was almost like someone had placed it there for a photo opportunity.

Beyond the pull cart, farther into the field, was a small rectangular structure, slightly larger than an outhouse, painted white and topped with a small onion dome. The side facing us had a rectangular opening with locked security bars. Behind the metal bars was a curtain. I asked Krishan about it and he said it was a temple where the Dalit caste could worship. I nearly fell out of my chair. "Even the places of worship are separate? Theirs is in a field and the structure is less than a tenth of the size of your temple?"

Before I moved to India, people had told me that India would rock the foundation of everything I thought of as normal. I had lived as a Peace Corps volunteer in West Africa and had seen many things that were exotic. Years later, I had worked in Cairo, where I had also experienced many things that were unique, including an unfamiliar, although still Abrahamic, religion. India blew those differences away.

This rocked my foundation. I just assumed that all religions were about equality and helping the less fortunate. Seeing the two distinctly different temples in this village forced me to think otherwise. While the government was supporting affirmative action, the Hindu religion supported the separation of classes. I started to do the math. India was about 80 percent Hindu. The population was about 1.2 billion. Eighty percent of that was just under a billion. For about one seventh of the world population, this social structure of inequality was the norm.

I asked Krishan about the interpretation on Hinduism that I had made from my visit to the museum months earlier. He told me that, generally, I had made a correct interpretation. That is, working through one's dharma is the work of the individual, and one should not interfere with another's journey. To a purist, if one was meant to suffer in this lifetime, they should be permitted to suffer. However, he also reminded me that Hinduism has as many interpretations as it has gods. Hinduism grew by absorbing the gods and beliefs of each village that came in the path of its expansion. He could cite examples of certain gods showing charity by giving alms to the poor. Making a generalization about Hinduism is as difficult as making a generalization about India. For everything that we can say about India, the opposite can be said. Perhaps that was true for Hinduism as well.

The next morning, Sandeep and Balbir came to the house to send us off. They walked us up to the main road, carrying our bags, and waited with us until the bus came. We snapped photos, and I made sure to put my arm across Sandeep's shoulder. I was sorry that he had to experience prejudice and wanted him to see this American didn't give two hoots about his caste. Krishan reminded me that things were getting better for them, especially in terms of treatment by the younger generation. They're touching them and befriending them but still not marrying them. Krishan added that the mayor of his village was from the Dalit caste, likely a product of the affirmative action.

While at the bus station where we changed buses, a man inquired about me to Krishan. The man wanted to speak to me and wondered if I spoke Punjabi. He wanted to know why I was there and if I was married.

Krishan explained the purpose of our trip and that I was unmarried. The man asked why I hadn't married. I told Krishan to tell him I was waiting for the right person, and then to ask if he had any daughters whom I should consider. They continued in Punjabi for a few minutes, the man glancing at me at times, and then the man smiled and said good-bye to me. Krishan told me the man took me seriously about the marriage proposal and asked what caste I was in. "Really? Doesn't he understand that I'm not from here? How did you answer that?" Krishan told me the man probably didn't know much beyond his village and thought the entire world fit into the Indian caste system. Krishan told him that I was of a Christian caste of sorts. That seemed to work and was enough to end the marriage idea.

My last weeks in Delhi involved many of the typical closure activities necessary for moving. Securing movers, attending send-off parties, picking up last-minute items, writing a letter of reference for Mrs. Kaur so that she might be able to work for the teacher who would be replacing me, and so forth. In the past few months I had been "building my raft" for my return and planning my life back in the United States.

Part of that closure was knowing that I wouldn't have my weekly dinners with Krishan. I would miss his friendship, company, and all of the learning experiences I had through him. He wanted to have me over for dinner and to meet his parents. It, of course, was a lovely evening, and in the end, Krishan presented me with a gift: an Indian wall hanging depicting a woman in a forest with a deer. It was made by gluing colored sand onto the paper. Beautiful, and so gracious of Krishan.

In our last days together, Krishan and I had watched several Indian movies together. As he could do so well, he explained anything I didn't understand. I asked Krishan if he had ever seen *The Sound of Music*. Not only had he not seen it, he had never heard of it! OK, I had a mission. I was not leaving India until he saw one of our best films. We positioned ourselves on the queen bed in my second bedroom and put my laptop on a pillow between us. He loved it! He was laughing and then crying and then laughing again when he saw that the nuns had taken the spark plugs from the Nazi cars.

I had decided to take some of India back with me and set about to use the shipping allowance that the school offered. The expat community had several seasoned shoppers, and they were delighted to help me with my goal, often taking me to their favorite artisan store. They were expert hagglers and therefore well respected by the shopkeepers, who would always offer a cup of chai before discussing a sale. Shopping in India was a hobby that many expats enjoyed and was usually included in our weekend plans.

I bought a large book cabinet that was handmade using darkly stained teak wood and well-ornamented wrought iron that was likely recycled from some torn-down balcony in Delhi. I purchased a tall but thin buffet cabinet with a green marble top along with an antique, round, mixed rosewood and teak end table with a white marble top. I had purchased a huge, heavy, brass elephant along with a smaller baby elephant. In my last week in Delhi, I decided to make one more round of the government artisan shops in downtown New Delhi.

Each of the twenty-nine states in India had a "government store" that sold artifacts created in that particular state. The stores were adjacent to one another and filled two city blocks. Uttar Pradesh is the state that is home to the Taj Mahal, so that store was a great one to pick up the white marble figurines or boxes that had semiprecious stones set into them. The Tamil Nadu state store was known for its bronze figurines, usually of Hindu gods. Haryana is not a well-known state, with no tourist attractions to speak of, but nonetheless it had a store that was on the very end of the two-block-long row of shops. I knew I had to get something from that shop but wondered what they would have. It was a small shop and was mostly filled with embroidered textiles, made by a women's group and whose proceeds would go to improving opportunities for women in Haryana. Since there wasn't much to choose from, my choice was easy: an intricately embroidered silk ruby-red wall hanging. In the rectangular center were geometric designs in jewel-toned threads accented with beige and the occasional plastic mirror sewn into the design. Beautiful! I would remember the Kassana cousins when I looked at this on my condo wall in Florida.

Chapter Fourteen

I've been back in the United States for four school years now. While I was overseas, I always missed my family and the United States in general. It felt good to be home.

In the past, whenever my flight from overseas pulled up to a gate at Chicago's O'Hare International Airport, my usual destination, I would love hearing the official greeting through the plane's intercom system, "Welcome to the United States of America." Sometimes it gave me goose bumps. I'd think, "I'm home now." People all over the world wanted to live in the United States, and so did I. To name a few pluses, the United States was relatively peaceful and had clean air, clean food, excellent hospitals, friendly people, and great sights for me to see. And I could eat beef and pork any time I wanted! One expat teacher in Delhi used to say that when she was stateside, she'd eat an "ABC diet": "Anything But Chicken," as chicken was the only easily available meat in India.

Of course, I got right onto securing a job and settling down in Fort Lauderdale. India was becoming a distant memory, but I found myself looking more closely at the Indian Americans I saw, as well as at the Indian tourists. I often saw ethnic Indians lunching at Chipotle. It had fresh ingredients and lots of vegetarian options; it made sense to me. I still try not to stare at them eating their lunch, but the sight of them brings back a rush of fond memories of my friends in Punjab.

When I really want to step back into India, I go to Indian restaurants. From the background Indian music to the bright, white-teeth smiles of the waitstaff, I am enchanted. I wonder about the state from which the waitstaff emigrated. Were they from a village? Were they married? If so, were their weddings arranged and as elaborate as I had experienced? Had they checked the sex of their first child to ensure it was a male? To which god did they give their devotion? And *why was there no chapati in the buffet line?*

I was so excited when my shipment from India arrived. When the movers finished unpacking everything, I sent them off, closed my condo door, and got to work placing each piece, relishing the process. As I did that, the fond memories of purchasing the item and the friends with whom I was shopping came to my mind. Sometimes I'd remember the shopkeeper who sold it to me.

Those were my physical "takeaways" from India, my souvenirs. The word "souvenir" comes from the French meaning "remembrance." These items would help me do just that. I also had many photos that I snapped, along with the many that my Haryana friends took. While I was first put off by their snatching of my camera from my hands, I was now very appreciative of the many photos they snapped with it. As India is arguably the most photogenic country on the planet, it would have been a shame to come back with too few photos.

More than the trinkets, furniture, and photos, my greatest treasure is what India taught me that I have now incorporated into my life back home. I believe that each of us carries a large suitcase of culture with us wherever we go. Often we don't know what's in it until we meet someone who has different cultural experiences. Then we say to ourselves, "Oh, we never did that in my family growing up," or "How cool; it makes so much sense to do it that way." What I've tried to do with my years of interacting with different cultures is to remove from my suitcase any of my cultural norms that weren't serving me well and to replace them with what I've learned from other cultures that made good sense and would add value to my life.

Below are some of the many cultural "takeaways" from India that I've added to my cultural suitcase.

Ghee. Ghee is nondairy, and it is considered to be healthy fat that is filled with high amounts of vitamins A and K. Yes, butter is now good for us, at least, according to the Atkins, Paleo, and the other slow-carb and evolutionary diets. Butter smokes at too low a temperature for frying, so why not use ghee? When a recipe calls for melted butter, why not just use ghee, as it's already in liquid form? Add it to smoothies or on top of a bowl of fruit. Ghee dripped over fruit makes every bite taste like you're eating a fruit pie. And it's good for you!

Taking your shoes off at the door. While this was commonplace in most of the world, and in my two previous host countries in Africa, Cameroon and Egypt, before India I had not added this custom to my suitcase. In India, the streets often had dried feces from dogs, cows, and, yes, humans. It made so much sense to remove one's shoes in India. Some cultures, especially Middle Eastern cultures, see the bottom of the shoe as the dirtiest part of our attire. Remember when George Bush had a shoe thrown at him? Exposing the bottom of the shoe or foot is the ultimate form of disrespect to elders in many cultures. Take your shoes off at the door: it's good for your feet, your floors and carpets, and the hygiene of your home.

Raw milk. If you're one of the lucky ones who can tolerate dairy items, give raw dairy products from grass-fed cattle a try. I alternate between buying raw yogurt, cheese, and kefir. Raw dairy products are loaded with many more vitamins and nutrients than pasteurized dairy products. And these days raw dairy products are increasingly available for purchase. Where I currently live, in Florida, the label must read "For Animal Consumption Only," wink, wink. Read up on it and give it a try.

Acceptance of differences: embrace multiculturalism. With the exception of the outdated caste system, India is accepting of diversity like no place on the planet. India for first timers can look like a parade of costumes and cultures. With twenty-nine states where people often dress according to their geographic region—for example, the occasional sadhu or guru in orange or red robes, the Muslim men with their prayer caps and flowing gowns, or Western clothes—and the various social castes and economic layers, India is far from homogeneous. I remember shopping with Eileen in an outdoor market and looking out of a tunnel of fabric at the shoppers who passed by the shop. Halloween in the United

States was the only time I had seen so many different costumes in front of me. With arguably every major religion represented (many founded in India), India raises a population of individuals who are used to interacting with people different from them. While the constitution declares Hindi and English (with a footnote to be phased out over fifteen years) as the official languages, it also allows each state to declare official languages. And they do. And if that isn't enough, most of the languages are written in different scripts. The ten-rupee note translates "ten rupees" into no less than fifteen languages, *each in a different script*. If there was any country in the world that could teach the rest how to live together, it would be Mother India.

Eating a little dirt not only won't kill us, it actually will help us. A lot has been written recently about the overuse of antibiotics, antibacterial soaps, and hand sanitizers. While they seem to be the right things to use, they are preventing us from adapting to the multitude of bacteria that would otherwise make us more robust and resilient to infections. After eating unwashed fruits and vegetables in India, I no longer wash my vegetables before cooking them. When I've been tempted to take an antibiotic, I've refused because I didn't want to lose the good bacteria I had built up in India. Thankfully, I've not taken antibiotics in the five years I've been back.

Being less of a bleeding heart might actually do more good. If my interpretation of this aspect of Hinduism is even partially correct, my takeaway would be to balance the Hindu "fix yourself and don't interfere with others' dharma" with the Abrahamic philosophy of charity—that is, the obligation to help others. While I'm sure all would agree that societal structures should be in place to allow all to prosper, giving handouts can create a society of "learned helplessness," which is good for nobody.

Spices. Yes, spice it up! Is pumpkin pie the only time you pull out the exotic spices? Turmeric is getting a lot of attention for its anti-inflammatory benefits. Add it to scrambled eggs. If you don't like the taste, take a daily capsule of it to reap its enormous health benefits. Have you ever tried the fragrant cardamom? In India it is best known for its use in rice pudding, and it is a standard, of course, in chai. Give it a try. And what about the array of curries? There's more than one type of black pepper. Explore. Make it a goal to research recipes that call for the ingredients that brought world attention—and the British, Portuguese, French, and Dutch—to the subcontinent. Warm them in the pan to enliven the flavors before adding the meat or vegetables. Be sure to keep the lid on when warming mustard seeds, as they pop like corn!

Bollywood. While I hesitate to include Bollywood as a takeaway, it can't go without mention. Westerners cannot watch the films through the same lenses as we would a Hollywood film. Indian films are family films, usually with some variation of boy meets girl, conflict ensues, and then all is resolved in the end. Add to this Broadway-style dancing (sometimes exact choreography copied from our films), colorful costumes, and a rain scene where all get happily drenched. Give one a try!

Indian music. Like most Asian music, Indian music is an acquired taste for Westerners. Getting used to the high-pitched female voice is the greatest hurdle. This trait likely evolved from having to sing outdoors where acoustics didn't project the voices (a higher pitch would carry voices farther). Thankfully, A. R. Rahman's recent music bridges the gap for the Western ear. Westerners who saw *Slumdog Millionaire* will recognize the theme from that film, for which he won two Academy Awards and a Golden Globe. Start with his Signature Collection and work your way backward or just stick to the Western movie albums he's made.

Male-male intimacy. Sexual intimacy between men is appropriate for some, but nonsexual intimacy is natural and healthy for all men. In much of the world, men embrace, kiss, hold hands, sleep in the same bed together, lean against one another, giggle together, and generally have no phobias about physical contact with another man. For some reason, American men go to extremes to avoid any and all of that. Perhaps it's an extension of the strong, macho, cowboy persona that American men are burdened to carry. One can only wonder what the psychological implications are on American men of not being able to be physical with one another.

Squat sit. Sadly, most Westerners older than twenty-five years can't do this. Sometimes known as the "third-world squat," most people in the less industrialized countries can do this effortlessly and can keep the position for an extended period of time. Understandably, the arch of your back created by the squat sit does wonders for your spine. Call it a stretch and add it to your workout.

Squat when you use the toilet. There are several products available that adapt to Western toilets. Squatting on a toilet allows for complete elimination and is said to reduce the risk of colon cancer and hemorrhoids. Our ancestors and the majority of today's world population excrete in this position; why shouldn't we? At the least, check out the Squatty Potty commercial. It is humorous and may just convince you to give it a try.

Friendship. The most important thing I brought back were the friend-ships I made by having an open mind and an open heart. Strangers embraced me with both because I gave them the opportunity. They will-ingly gave me their friendship without any motive other than enjoying my company. The warm embraces, generosity, and genuine laughter of the Haryana cousins will live in my heart forever. The insights given to me by Krishan will make me a better person. Mrs. Kaur fed me, and Mr. Singh and others safely transported me around Punjab.

Keeping an open heart attracts other open hearts. While not unique to my time in the Punjab, it's as true here as anywhere. If I've succeeded in the previous pages, this takeaway requires no explanation.

Namaste.

About the Author

Author Peter O'Neil has been intrigued by language and culture since his childhood in Wilmette, Illinois. He turned his interest into action, joining the US Peace Corps to volunteer in a remote mountain village in Cameroon.

While there, he discovered his passion for teaching math and the joy he finds meeting and befriending locals.

Since then, his career has taken him to classrooms around the world, including Venezuela, Cairo, Paris, and, most recently, the Punjab, India.

Made in the USA
San Bernardino, CA
18 November 2016